Other Books by Barbara Ensrud

American Vineyards

Wine with Food

The Pocket Guide to Cheese

The Pocket Guide to Wine

Best Wine Buys for $12 and Under

Villard
New York
1995

Best Wine Buys for $12 and Under

A Guide for the Frugal Connoisseur

Barbara Ensrud

Villard Books is a registered trademark of Random House, Inc.

This is a revised edition of *Best Wine Buys for $10 or Less* by Barbara Ensrud, which was originally published by Villard Books in 1991.

Library of Congress Cataloging-in-Publication data is available

ISBN 679-75662-0

Manufactured in the United States of America
Book design by J. K. Lambert
9 8 7 6 5 4 3 2

For

Allen and Marily,
Betty and Gil,
Bob and Kay

good friends
and savvy wine
buyers

Acknowledgments

I wish to express special thanks to my agent, Charlotte Sheedy, who saw the need for this book and prodded me to do it; and to my editor, Emily Bestler, for her enthusiasm, patience, and guidance in bringing the first edition to fruition.

Many years of contacts throughout the wine world have made this book possible. I am grateful to all of them—but especially to those who are dedicated to providing good wine at moderate prices for the American wine drinker.

Contents

Introduction

Drinking good wine can still be a wallet-busting proposition these days, but now more than ever it doesn't have to be. In the years since the first edition of this book appeared, American wine drinkers have become more value conscious. Notice that I said *value* conscious, not just cost conscious. People want bargains, to be sure, but they aren't necessarily looking for the cheapest wine available. Any of us are delighted to find a smashing little wine like Spain's Monastrell-Mourvèdre for $6 or a fresh, dry Rosé de Syrah from the south of France for $5. People seem willing to ante up $7 or $9, even $11 or $12 for a wine that's really worth it in terms of quality and style. Wine importers and distributors are bending over backwards to find such wines and make them available because this price category —$7 to $12—is the engine that drives the wine market today.

It's fine to splurge on $15, $20, or $40 wines when you feel like it, or when a special occasion merits it, but if you like to drink wine fairly regularly, prices like that can mount up to a small fortune fast. Even owners of lavish cellars like to know of bargains for everyday drinking. I know people who could pull forth a Château Lafite or Cheval-Blanc—mature and ready to drink—every night of the week. Truly great wines like these are serious and dramatic; they demand attention, you don't just quaff them down—you have to take note of all the complexities of aroma and character that make them the rare and costly creatures that they are. Even the owners of wonderfully stocked cellars aren't necessarily in the mood for an eventful wine *every* night.

Great wines can provide thrilling moments for the wine lover. (In fact, I insist on such moments at least once a week!) Most of us, however, are not looking for a "Great Experience" every time we open a bottle. We just want something that tastes good with our food, something that is enjoyable to drink. Some bargain wines can be more than that, though—like the spectacular $6 Cabernet from Chile that's more drinkable than some Bordeaux at thrice the price, or the Italian Rosso di Montalcino that costs a third of what its more illustrious cousin goes for.

Wine-pricing is capricious, and often bears no relation to the quality of what is inside the bottle. A lot of wineries—in this country and abroad—arbitrarily set the price of a given bottle based on how they want it to be perceived by the public and by critics, regardless of the quality of the grapes used to make it. Image-pricing, it's called. By the same token, there are excellent wines available that are underrated, wines that simply can't command the higher prices their quality merits. Such are the ways of the marketplace—it teems with quite ordinary stuff selling at highly inflated prices, while wine just as good, sometimes better, can be had for a song.

Price is, in fact, a spurious guide to drinking well. You don't always get what you pay for, and it's easy to make mistakes if you don't know what you're doing. This is as true for cheap wines as for those that are expensive or overpriced. There are hundreds of wines available for under $10, and dozens priced at $2.99 to $5.99 a bottle. Much of it is dreck.

Some of it, however, is very good indeed—in fact, it's amazing the number of good, drinkable wines available, all well under $10. The new $12 limit offers even more options. This book is an attempt to separate the wheat from the chaff—concentrating, of course, on the *wheat,* the good stuff, the *consistently* good stuff.

This book's approach differs from those of other buying guides in two significant ways. First, it discusses the types of wine and recommends producers rather than individual bottles of a specific vintage, and, second, there are no numerical ratings.

I find it frustrating to read guides that rate wines of a given vintage only to find that the wines in question are actually no longer available. This is especially true of inexpensive wines, most of which are intended for drinking when they come on the market. By the time the book is out, a new vintage has appeared. It's different with more expensive wines like classified Bordeaux; several vintages of Château Haut-Brion or Palmer, say, are often available simultaneously. In any case such wines are usually bought and cellared, so that individual vintage ratings for a specific wine have validity over a long period of time.

I have chosen instead to recommend wines that are of reliable quality on a consistent basis. Of what use is it to recommend the Beaulieu 1994 Beau Tour Cabernet Sauvignon if the wine that will be in stores when this book is published will be the '95? Or, if you read it a year from now, the '96?

It seems to me much more useful to know that, year in and year out, BV Beau Tour is an excellent buy—you don't have to buy a new edition of this guide next year to know that. This is true for a great many wines in the $12-and-under range because the producers recommended strive for consistent style and quality year to year. This book will not be totally out of date in a year— unless all herein suddenly cave in to compromise and mediocrity. Not likely, I'm thinking.

As for numerical ratings, I know they provide a quick clue to a wine's quality, but I've never really liked the notion of reducing wine to a cipher. It wouldn't work with this format anyway, since such ratings must be for individual wines of a given vintage. Everything recommended here offers good to excellent drinking. The information I offer is really only a starting point, because new wines at this level are coming onto the market all the time.

It gives me great pleasure to share the discoveries I've made through persistent tasting. If you keep up with newsletters and peruse wine periodicals and weekly wine columns in your local newspaper, many of these wines will already be familiar to you. Those of you who enjoy good wine but don't always have the time or inclination to chase after the various sources of information, however, may find yourselves referring to this guide frequently. Look up the wine you're curious about—if the name is under Recommended Producers, it's because the wine has proven consistently good and you can buy with confidence.

My objective here is to concentrate on great wine buys for $12 and under. Consequently some very nice wines don't make the cut—Dolcetto for $15 instead of the $9 or $10 that it used to be; ditto certain Barbera d'Alba and Pinot Grigio, as well as some Chardonnays, Merlots, and Zinfandels from California. Interestingly, though, the competition for shelf space and pressure to sell (there really is an awful lot of wine out there) bring on some surprising price reductions. Many of the wines that at full markup would be $14 or $16 can often be found for $12 or less. This is where it pays to seek out a compatible wineshop. Read on.

HOW TO USE THIS BOOK

The book is arranged geographically by country, and within each country the wines are listed according to how they are best known—in some cases by region (such as Bordeaux), in others by grape variety (Chardonnay), type (Rosso di Montalcino), or occasionally producer (Boutari), whichever is the most informative. A few symbols indicate special situations as follows:

- ✪ Superbuy, outstanding wine for the price
- ✳ Excellent value
- ♦ Wines that at full markup would be over $12 but are frequently found marked down or discounted
- ♥ Perceptible sweetness in wine types normally considered dry, such as Chardonnay
- ■ No oak in wines where oak aging is common

For unfamiliar terms, check the Glossary, page 173.

Best
Wine Buys
for $12
and Under

1

The Wineshop of the 1990s

The decade of the nineties appears to favor consumers, with sizable inventories of wine from a series of remarkably good vintages. As long as the pipeline is full, there will be pressure in the market to move wine—prices, particularly for wines in the $10 to $15 range, may well soften over the next few years, putting better wines back within reach of everyday drinking. People are drinking less, and while it is true that they are trading up, there is a limit to what they will spend on a regular basis.

One of the things I strongly encourage everyone to do is to make more intelligent—and enjoyable—use of a good wineshop. It's there for you, make it work for you. Too many consumers are intimidated by wineshops. Confronted by thousands of bottles, they have no idea how to go about choosing a wine. Usually they settle for a familiar name, or one they've seen advertised or heard about from a friend. Normally assertive people can turn timid in a wineshop, afraid to appear ignorant or unsophisticated. In some stores, it is true, the staff can be dismissive if you aren't looking for $40 Bordeaux or $20 Cabernets. Attitudes are changing, though, and the better stores are making every effort to become user-friendly.

The nineties have already demonstrated that a new era in wine retailing is well under way. In previous decades we saw the evolution of liquor store into wineshop—it may be a huge warehouse like Sam's Wine Warehouse in Chicago, or Trader Joe or The Wine House in Los Angeles. Often it's a wine-and-food emporium like Martin Wine Cellar in New Orleans, or A Southern Season in Chapel Hill, where you can shop for dinner *and* the wine to go with it. Today, every major metropolitan area has at least one and probably several such stores (see A Few Good Shops, page 175), which stock an amazing choice of wines. Even smaller cities and suburban areas now have good wineshops. They get better as store personnel learn more about wine and discover the rewards of being as helpful to customers as they can—steering them to good values, matching wine with menus for entertaining, and making them feel welcome and at home in the store.

Whatever its size, atmosphere, or decor, the wineshop of today has become a center of wine-oriented activity, a lively source of information and exchange. In states where on-premise tasting is permitted, retailers often hold regular tastings. By all means, check this out in your area; tasting is unquestionably the best way to find out what you really like. If your local shop holds regular tastings, they can be a wonderful way to experiment with new wines—expensive ones as well as bargains. At Schaefer's in the suburbs of Chicago, for instance, Saturday afternoon tastings always include some of the better, more expensive wines. In December, Calvert Woodley Liquors in Washington, D.C., holds sparkling wine tastings, pouring several of the top brands. These are very popular events; people try a range of Champagnes, exchange views about them, browse about the store for other holiday needs, and have a great time.

GET TO KNOW YOUR WINE MERCHANT

Wine merchants are a lot more knowledgeable than they used to be. A good wine merchant tastes constantly—probably as much as most wine writers do—knows his product, and makes sure his staff is knowledgeable, too. He (or she) can be a great resource. Don't be intimidated because you feel you don't know a lot about wine. If he has any sense of salesmanship, he will want to steer you to the best possible values for your money so you will come back. Yes, he undoubtedly has plenty of customers who spend a lot of money on wine, but he cannot rely on big spenders alone. He needs a broad clientele that keeps coming back. Besides, you may one day be a bigger customer than you are now.

Keeps coming back is a key phrase: It's why he needs to try to please you. In a national survey of wineshops, most merchants said that what they wanted to be known for was *service,* so let's hold them to it. If someone is dismissive or intimidates you in any way, confront him with it, or go to another store and perhaps explain *why* you left the first one. If there isn't another, complain to your local wine writer, or write to *The Wine Spectator* (or to me).

The new breed of wine retailers, however, recognizes that customers who are pleased with the guidance they get begin to take more interest in wine and become eager to try different wines and broaden their horizons. It can be very useful to establish a kind of rapport with a retailer or someone on the staff. As they get to know what you like and what your wine requirements are, they can more readily suggest the kinds of wines that would please you.

Wilfred Wong, wine buyer at Tower Market in San Francisco, says it all comes down to trust. "The bottom line is trust," says Wong. "If people don't trust what you stock, then forget it. People get suspicious when they see a wine marked down, for instance. 'What's wrong with it?' they ask. If you want a loyal clientele, you have to taste the wines yourself, so you know what you're offering and can stand behind it."

USING YOUR WINESHOP:
WHAT TO LOOK FOR

Specials and Markdowns. Wineshops like to feature specials, especially if they advertise in the local newspaper. Sometimes these are called loss leaders, wines the store makes little or no profit on just to attract attention—the prospect of a bargain always lures customers. I saw Château Meyney 1990, normally $17 to $19 at full markup, for $11.95 in one shop—it's a good buy at $17 but a rare find under $12.

Even the best shops will eventually mark down wines they can't move—like lesser vintages of Bordeaux or wines that may be very good but didn't quite catch on. Sometimes there are real gems to be had.

But *whoa!* I am *not* saying that all wines on special are good buys. *Far from it.* A 1987 Hermitage for $12? A '91 Meursault for $10? Beware. These wines normally cost three times those amounts. If either is really good, chances are the retailer would have quietly mentioned it to one of his best customers who he knows loves Meursault. Not invariably, of course; maybe it really is a terrific wine, and a great buy. If it isn't, and he values you as a customer, he will steer you to something better at the same price.

I actually saw in one reputable Manhattan wineshop, in 1990, a bin of 1979 Côtes-du-Rhône. 1979? Totally puzzled, I asked the proprietor about it. Côtes-du-Rhône is usually a wine to drink within two to three years, maybe six or seven for Guigal (the top producer), but eleven!?? He looked a little embarrassed and admitted that a distributor had "discovered" a couple of leftover cases sitting around, and he had bought it for fifty cents on the dollar. Interesting, I thought, and he's selling it for $5.99 a bottle. "Is it any good?" I asked. Again, slight hesitation. "Well," he said, with a shrug, "it's a little tired."

By the same token I have seen four- to five-year-old Beaujolais, or even Beaujolais *nouveau,* believe it or not, sitting around on sale. Even at $2.99, this is no deal. It's old, it's tired, it's lost its fruit. I would venture to say, in fact, beware of anything on sale for $3 or less. It could be all right—certainly some of the Romanian or Bulgarian table wines that go for that amount are perfectly decent, if not great. But always try a bottle before you buy such a wine in quantity.

Direct Imports. Some retailers travel to wine regions regularly and seek out wines they can import directly and offer to their customers as exclusives at low prices. These can be excellent value for casual occasions or for large parties. Sherry-Lehmann in Manhattan, one of the first shops in this country to specialize in wine way back in the 1950s, has had enormous success for years with its $4.99 Cler Blanc, a delightful little quaff from the Loire Valley. Recently they added an agreeable "house" red made in the Rhône Valley, which they sell for the same reasonable price. Some shops make it a point to have several such wines; they are worth checking out, and often more interesting and stylish than jug wines.

In-Store Tastings. Attend these regularly if you can, *if* you find them helpful and fun. They should be both. Such events are not legal in some states, unfortunately. In others, wineshops can sponsor such events or hold them jointly with restaurants, but they aren't permitted in the store itself.

Newsletters. Get on the mailing list. Many wineshops publish catalogs or newsletters that are enormously helpful in letting you know about new arrivals, special sales, new books, tastings, wine dinners, and other events. Most newsletters are informative. Some are very amusing and entertaining—like the one put out by Glenn Bardgett and Geoffrey Brooke of the Wine Cellar in

St. Louis. Punsters, these two, but I laugh as much as I groan at some of their wordplay on wine names.

Some shops also have wine books, newsletters by wine critics, and other periodicals available for customers to peruse. Take a look if they do; such sources are a good way to pick up tips on what's new and what's hot.

Half-bottles. Always check out the half-bottle section. It may well offer the opportunity for something good that costs twice as much for a full bottle. For instance, $9 or $10 can get you one of those Chardonnays, Cabernets, Bordeaux, or Rhônes that sell for $15 to $20 in a 750-milliliter bottle. It is now legal to sell 500 milliliter (half-liter) bottles, which will give two people two generous glasses each. The 500s haven't quite caught on yet, but they may yet become very popular with consumers.

Wineries, restaurants, and wineshops often consider half-bottles a nuisance, requiring special handling and extra expense. But they offer just the right amount on occasion—especially for singles but also for couples who maybe just want to enjoy one glass each with dinner on a week night.

It's important to know, however, that half-bottles age faster than regular bottles—anything that's been around too long could well be fading or over the hill. Don't buy a half-bottle of four-year-old Muscadet, for example. Again, ask about the wine if you aren't sure—and if it turns out to be disappointing, tell the store. Or take it back the next day. I know it's not easy to do that, but you don't have to make a scene. Express surprise that it wasn't good, and ask the owner or salesman if he knows why.

Browse. Take time to browse in wineshops when
you can, whether you're prepared to buy at that
moment or not. The owner won't mind, and
doing so is very instructive. You begin to get familiar with wine names (which most consumers
say is their biggest problem: They can't remember the names of the wines they've tasted somewhere and liked). You observe what people
are buying, hear what's being recommended.
Chances are you'll even see a bottle or two you
want to try—and do it. As long as you're not
spending a fortune, this is the best possible way
to discover what you like and what you *don't* like
—which is also important.

Buying Wine. Whenever you can, buy by the
case, especially if you are buying a wine you
know you like. A great opportunity to do so is
when you're buying for a party. Buy a few more
bottles than you actually need. If you do this peri-
odically, you will find yourself building a modest
collection before you know it. You'll soon see
how handy it is to have wine on hand when the
right moment presents itself unexpectedly. You
might want to buy a case of all the same wine, or
a mixed case of three or four wines, or six. Buying this way lets you get ahead of the game a bit,
so that you don't get caught short and have to
make an emergency run to the wine store. There
are other advantages as well—buying by the case
can be cheaper, for instance. If the wine isn't
already on sale, you may get up to 10 percent off
for buying a case, the equivalent of a free bottle.

Discount Stores. No question about it, wine
prices are rising across the board, especially imports. And despite our expanding our limit to
$12, some wines have shot beyond that and had

to be dropped. Strong economies in Europe, a weaker American dollar, and an increased global demand for good wine have all contributed to the situation, which is likely to continue through the decade. Discount stores provide a kind of buffer against this. Because they buy in such huge quantities, they can afford to cut their profit margins per bottle. This makes a huge difference sometimes in wines priced from $8 to $15. The savings can be somewhat less on more expensive wines. For Bordeaux and Burgundy, in fact, nondiscount stores may offer better buys, particularly on first offerings for new vintages. This is because wine merchants that have long-standing relationships with top châteaux or estates are often able to get in large orders at the earliest price. Replacement costs for wines from good vintages are always higher.

Go to a wine supermarket like Liquor Barn or Cost Plus if you know exactly what you want to buy. If you are less certain, go to a store that stocks less but is known for quality. There, no matter what you buy, you are likely to get more carefully chosen wines and better service. Most wine lovers who can do so shop both places. Sometimes it is worth a few dollars more to get the kind of individual attention, advice, and services (like free delivery) that smaller stores offer.

2

France

The world's most expensive wines are made in France, but it also produces prototypes for some of the very best moderate-priced wines. You can still drink well for $6 to $9 with the likes of Beaujolais, Muscadet, Pinot Blanc, Côtes-du-Rhône, a dollar or so more for wines like Mâcon-Villages, Saint-Véran, even quite respectable Bordeaux among the *Cru bourgeois* and certain proprietary brands.

In the southern regions of France, long known for huge quantities of mediocre wine, tremendous retrenchment is under way, with new plantings of varieties like Cabernet Sauvignon, Merlot, Syrah, and Chardonnay. Stylish new wines from regions like Provence, the Ardèche, Languedoc, and the southwest are creating a lot of excitement. Dozens of new labels have appeared that include terrific values.

French wines traditionally have place names—

region (Bordeaux), village (Sancerre), or vineyard (La Tâche, or Château Latour). The prac-
tice of naming wines for grape variety (Riesling,
Chardonnay, Pinot Blanc) formerly existed only
in Alsace. In recent years French producers, not-
ing the U.S. market for varietal wines, have en-
thusiastically leaped on the bandwagon with
moderately priced Chardonnay, Cabernet, Merlot, and Sauvignon Blanc. It's a category to be
wary of because quality varies considerably, but
there are plenty such wines worth recommend-
ing.

This chapter is arranged alphabetically by region—Bordeaux, the Loire Valley—then subdi-
vided into the leading wines of the region.
Varietal wines are treated separately.

ALSACE

Alsace is the only fine-wine region of France that
makes use of varietal names. As a whole, the
region produces wine of higher overall quality
than any other in France. Alsace produces
mostly white wines: Riesling, Gewurztraminer,
Pinot Blanc, Sylvaner, Pinot Gris (also known as
Tokay d'Alsace), and Muscat. What is notable
is that they are dry, a surprise (even a shock
sometimes) to wine drinkers used to sweet Rieslings and Gewurz. Alsace wines age superbly—
in fact, Riesling and Gewurztraminer are usually
better in their third or fourth years, and they can
easily last a decade if well stored.

Large shippers like Trimbach, Hugel, Leon
Beyer, and Dopff "Au Moulin" established the
high standards for Alsace wines, making them
available at moderate prices. In the last decade
individual growers like Domaine Weinbach,

Zind-Humbrecht, and a few others have risen to prominence with truly remarkable Riesling, Gewurztraminer, Muscat, and Pinot Gris. Prices for these limited-quantity wines have also risen, steeply in some cases. Some Gewurztraminer and Pinot Gris are well over $12 a bottle now. Riesling and Pinot Blanc, however, remain excellent values, particularly from the large shippers.

One fact in the consumer's favor is that Alsace wines are not as well known or understood in the United States as other French wines, so you may find them marked down or on special at prices within the $12 limit. With this in mind, some producers are included with ♦ for wines that are just over the limit at full markup.

Gewurztraminer

The most distinctive of Alsace wines, intensely fragrant, with sweet spicy/floral aromas that are quite different from any other wine. Bone-dry, it's not to everyone's taste, by any means. Alsace Gewurz cannot be compared to versions made elsewhere, which are usually sweet. Most of the best from Alsace now cost considerably more than $12, even those that aren't Reserves, thus the exclusion of excellent wines from Deiss, Josmeyer, Weinbach, and Zind-Humbrecht (though keep an eye out for markdowns).

Age: 2–3 years, can age and improve 5–10
Price: $8–10 +
Recommended Producers: Lucien Albrecht, E. Boeckel, Dopff "Au Moulin," Gustave Lorentz, J. L. Mader, René Muré, Ostertag, Pierre Sparr, Trimbach, A. Willm
Foods: A dramatic aperitif; excellent with foie gras and liver pâté; rich Oriental dishes like General

Tso's chicken and other deep-fried foods; can be
too overpowering for lighter dishes

Pinot Blanc

Fresh, crisp, and dry, Pinot Blanc is one of the
best Alsace values. In California it comes closer
to Chardonnay than here, where it is more neutral in character, brisk but fruity, very appealing
and quite versatile with food.

Age: 1–3 years
Price: $5–8
Recommended Producers: Adam, Leon Beyer, E.
    Boeckel, Marcel Deiss, Dopff "Au Moulin," Hugel
    Cuvée des Amours, Kuentz-Bas, Clos St. Landelin,
    Gustave Lorentz, Julien Meyer, Schlumberger,
    Schoffit ♦, Albert Selz, Pierre Sparr, Trimbach,
    A. Willm
Foods: Simply prepared fish, white meat chicken,
    seafood pastas, chicken or veal sausage, quiche;
    also excellent aperitif

Riesling

Probably the best-known Alsace wine, it is dry
and steely when quite young but softens as it
matures. I like Alsace Rieslings best at three to
four years, when the firmness has become more
supple and the wine's flowery fragrance is more
apparent. Younger Rieslings have the appealing
zest of green apples or citrus, with mouth-
watering acidity that gets the taste buds going.
Those recommended here represent excellent
value.

Age: 2–4 years, but some hold easily for 4–6, and
   can age to 10
Price: $7–10
Recommended Producers: Adam, Lucien Albrecht,
   Leon Beyer, E. Boeckel, Dopff "Au Moulin" ✳,
   Gustave Lorentz, J. L. Mader, Pierre Sparr,
   Trimbach, A. Willm
Foods: Ideal with Oriental foods, including Chinese,
   Thai, Vietnamese, Indian, and more versatile
   than Gewürztraminer; superb with broiled trout
   or sole, *coq au Riesling, choucroute* and other
   sausage dishes, roast pork, ham; an excellent
   aperitif

Sylvaner

Dry and agreeable, quite inexpensive, but too
often vapid in character; not recommended in
light of above values, which are more widely
available. The exceptions: Adam, Albert Selz,
Trimbach, Domaine Weinbach.

BERGERAC

This region east of Bordeaux produces stylish
red wines from Cabernet and Merlot and dry
whites from Sauvignon Blanc that offer excellent
value. A few more have made it to the United
States in recent years—they're well worth trying.

Age: 1–3 years for whites, 2–5 for reds
Price: $6–8
Recommended Producers: Château Calabre,
   Château Grinou, Domaine de la Jaubertie ✳,

Chateau Les Justices, Michel de Montaigne,
Château La Roche Combet
Foods: See Bordeaux Red and White

BORDEAUX (Red)

Bordeaux enjoyed a string of superb vintages in the 1980s (1986, 1988, and 1989, as well as 1990, 1991, and 1994). Prices have steadily risen also. Still, it is not as difficult as it might seem to find good, drinkable Bordeaux for under $12 and even $10. There are numerous properties known as *petits châteaux* that offer excellent value, the most consistent of which are listed below.

Also included are wines from satellite areas adjacent to the premiere districts of the Médoc, Pomerol, Saint-Emilion, and Graves. These regions—such as Fronsac, Canon-Fronsac, Côtes de Bourg, Côtes de Blaye, Côtes de Castillon, Côtes de Francs—have undergone considerable renovation and replanting in the last decade. Several good wines from these regions are included in the long list below, but value-conscious consumers should be aware that new ones continue to come along.

Listed here is a personal selection of wines that have shown consistent quality and style for several vintages. Usually blends of Merlot, Cabernet Sauvignon, and/or Cabernet Franc, these dry, firm reds emphasize fruit over depth; they have the character of fine Bordeaux but on a smaller scale, and they are ready to drink within two to five years. Note the Superbuys.

Best Bordeaux Vintages

1994	1988
1991	1986
1990	1985
1989	1985

Proprietary brands are listed in a separate category.

Age: 2–5 years, will go a decade in good vintages
Price: $7–10
Foods: Lamb, beef, duck, cheeses like Camembert, Port Salut, goat cheese
Recommended Châteaux (Wines with ♦ are over $12 at full markup but are frequently discounted):

Arnaud (Haut-Médoc)
Bacchus (Graves de Vayre)
Baret (Graves)
du Barry (Saint-Emilion)
Beaumont (Haut-Médoc)
Château Beau Séjour (Côtes de Castillon)
Bel Air (Haut-Médoc)
de Belcier ✪ (Côtes de Castillon)
Cabannieux (Graves)
Canon de Brem (Canon-Fronsac)
La Cardonne (Médoc)
de Carles (Fronsac)
Chantegrive ✪ (Graves)
Cormeil-Figeac (Saint-Emilion)
La Dauphine (Fronsac)
La Duchesse (Canon-Fronsac)
Fonneuve (Première Côtes de Bordeaux)
Fonplégade (Saint-Emilion)
La Fontaine (Fronsac)
de Francs (Côtes de Francs)
La Garde (Graves)
du Gazin (Fronsac)
Grandes Nauves (Lalande-Pomerol)
de La Grave (Bordeaux Supérieur)
Greysac (Haut-Médoc) ✪

La Grolet (Côtes de
Blaye)

Guiraud Cheval Blanc
(Côtes de Bourg)

Haut-Sociando (Côtes
de Blaye)

Jonquéyres (Bordeaux
Supérieur)

du Juge (Premières
Côtes de Bordeaux)

Larose-Trintaudon ✪
(Haut-Médoc)

Lestage (Listrac)

Loudenne
(Haut-Médoc)

Malescasse ♦
(Haut-Médoc)

du Mayne
(Haut-Médoc)

Meyney ♦
(Saint-Estephe)

Moulin Rouge (Côtes
de Castillon)

Perenne (Médoc)

Piron (Graves)

Pitray (Côtes de
Castillon)

Plagnac (Médoc)

Puy-Blanquet
(Saint-Emilion)

Puyguerrand (Côtes de
Francs)

Ramage La Batisse
(Médoc)

Reysson (Haut-Médoc)

Romefort (Haut
Médoc)

Saint-Marie
(Haut-Médoc)

Le Sartre (Graves)

Senéjac (Haut-Médoc)

Tayac Rubis (Côtes de
Bourg)

La Tuilerie (Graves)

Vieux Meyney
(Bordeaux)

Villars (Fronsac)

Proprietary Brands (Red and White)

Some excellent buys in proprietary brands have
emerged in recent years. They represent some
of the best bargains in red Bordeaux. Several top
châteaux—Cos d'Estournel, Ducru-Beaucaillou,
Lynch-Bages, among others—are producing simple but good-quality, immediately drinkable reds
that are excellent values.

Age: 2–4 years
Price: $5–8

Recommended Producers: **Château Beau-Rivages,
Château Bonnet, Canon Moueix, Jean Cordier,
Fondation 1725, Lauretan, Michel Lynch Rouge
✪, Maître d'Estournel, Mouton Cadet**

BORDEAUX (White, Dry)

Good, inexpensive dry white Bordeaux is somewhat more plentiful than formerly, but mostly
under proprietary labels, as listed below. The
region Entre-Deux-Mers produces mostly dry
white wines, which are gradually improving, but
a great many of them are mediocre. White Bordeaux is made from Sauvignon Blanc or Sauvignon blended with Sémillon, with the tart,
slightly herbaceous character that makes it difficult to drink except with food. Most are intended
for drinking early. My main complaint about
these wines is that they still tend to be oversulphured—except for those listed below.

Age: 1–3 years
Price: $6–10
Recommended Producers: **Château Bacchus,
Château Bertinerie, Bonnet, du Bordier,
Cabannieux, Doisy-Daene, Domaine Challon,
Dourthe Frères, Ducla, l'Etoile, Fondation 1725,
Château 'G,' Château du Juge, Château Launay,
Maître d'Estournel, du Mayne, Saint-Jovian,
Château Thieuley**

BEAUJOLAIS

Beaujolais is actually a district within the larger
appellation of Burgundy. These popular fruity
reds, often best when lightly chilled, are made

from the Gamay grape, however, not Pinot Noir, the grape used for red Burgundy. If you drive from Paris to Provence and the Côte d'Azur, the hills of Beaujolais begin to rise on your right south of Mâcon and continue to Lyons. Beaujolais is the quintessential quaffing wine, one of the best light reds for summer, and versatile with many types of food. Its charm derives from the generous and sometimes quite intense fruit of Gamay, hinting of ripe berries and spice. The thing to know about Beaujolais is that there are levels of quality, ranging from simple Beaujolais, the lightest, to Beaujolais-Villages and then the *crus*—wines named for the communes where the grapes are grown such as Brouilly, Fleurie, Moulin à Vent (listed under *Crus*). Beaujolais and Beaujolais-Villages are best consumed within a year, Villages somewhat longer. The *crus* can go two years for the lightest (Brouilly, Regnié), up to three or four for more substantial ones (Juliénas, Morgon, Moulin à Vent). Small amounts of Beaujolais Blanc and Rosé are also made in the region.

Beaujolais Nouveau. It is also important to know that Beaujolais *nouveau* (literally "new Beaujolais") is the first wine to become available after the harvest, released officially on the third Thursday of November. Very fruity, often highly perfumed with the scent of raspberries, it can be a delightful quaff and should always be lightly chilled. Originally, it served as a sort of stopgap, light, fruity wine intended for drinking only a few months until the year's wine (*Beaujolais de l'année*) became available in the spring. Today, half of the Beaujolais crop (excluding the *crus*) goes into *nouveau*. Shipped all over the world, it has become a bit heavier and more intense. Most *nouveau,* however, should be consumed by March or April following the vintage.

Beaujolais.

Wines labeled simply Beaujolais are the lightest of the region and not always the best value. In a ripe, sunny year, simple Beaujolais proves an excellent value, but most years Beaujolais-Villages (see) is a better buy. It is usually best when lightly chilled.

Age: Up to a year
Price: $5–7
Recommended Producers: Georges Duboeuf, Louis Jadot, Louis Latour

Beaujolais Blanc

A dry white made from Chardonnay grown in the Beaujolais region, mostly the northern part west of Mâcon. Similar to Mâcon-Villages but somewhat richer and not often seen in the United States.

Age: 1–2 years
Price: $8–10 +
Recommended Producers: J. P. Brun, Georges Duboeuf, Pierre Ferraud, Louis Jadot
Foods: Simple fish, chicken salad, cold meats, veal sausage; also a good dry aperitif

Beaujolais Nouveau

Not always the lightest in body, but certainly the fruitiest and most ephemeral of the Beaujolais. It can be delightful from Thanksgiving and through the winter. Buy it then; by April it has often lost its fresh appeal, though in some years it will hold up a few months longer. I'm appalled, however, when I see *nouveau* that is a year, two years, even *three* years old for sale in a wine-shop. *Avoid* such wines at any price. *Nouveau* is best lightly chilled, which makes the fruit snappier and fresher. Also, if you pay more than $7.49 for *nouveau,* you are paying too much.

Age: 2–6 months
Price: $5–7.50
Recommended Producers: Gabriel Aligne, B&G, Jean Bédin, Georges Duboeuf ✪, Pierre Ferraud, Sylvain Fessy, Jaffelin, Prosper Maufoux, Mommessin, Antonin Rodet
Foods: All types of casual fare, hamburgers, chicken wings, cold meats, saucissons and other sausages, cheeses mild or savory

---

Beaujolais Rosé

A dry, fruity rosé made from the Beaujolais grape, Gamay. Can be delightfully fresh, crisp, and appealing, but it is not often seen in the United States. Drink within a year. Best producer: Georges Duboeuf.

Beaujolais-Villages

Usually the best value in Beaujolais, fuller in body than simple Beaujolais, and fruitier. The grapes come from about thirty villages on the lower slopes north and west of Villefranche. Beaujolais's fruity charm is most freely expressed in Beaujolais-Villages. The best *nouveau* is often Villages.

Age: 12-18 months

Price: $5-8

Recommended Producers: Gabriel Aligne, B&G, Paul Beaudet, Jean Bédin, Joseph Drouhin, Georges Duboeuf ✪, Pierre Ferraud, Sylvain Fessy, Louis Jadot, Château de Lacarelle, Prosper Maufoux, Domaine Miolane, Mommessin, Domaine des Nugues, Joel Rochette, Antonin Rodet, Trenel

Foods: Same as for *nouveau*

The Crus

The term *cru* means "growth" and refers to a classified vineyard or specially defined area, in this case designated communes, or villages, of Beaujolais. It is the region's highest appellation in terms of quality. The wines have more body, more flesh, more intense fruit, and richer texture than simple Beaujolais or Villages. There are ten of them, and they vary somewhat in weight and intensity. Brouilly, Chiroubles, Côtes de Brouilly, and Regnié are the lightest of the *crus* in body and color, but a wonderful fruitiness is their main appeal. Fleurie, Juliénas, and Saint-Amour are deeper in color but juicy and flavorful. Fleurie, the most popular of the *crus,* has the most extravagant aromas of berryish fruit with a hint of spice and roses; it is also the most expensive, sometimes hitting $12 or $15 a bottle. The richest and darkest of the *crus* are Chénas, Morgon, and Moulin à Vent, the last occasionally almost Burgundian in character. These wines are somewhat more age-worthy. Moulin à Vent has been known to hold well for five to ten years.

Be careful when buying the *crus.* Initial markups can be high, especially for Fleurie, Morgon, and Moulin à Vent. Producers like Georges Duboeuf (dubbed the "king of Beaujolais" in France) make every effort to hold prices at $10 or under, but at current exchange rates many of the *crus* have pushed beyond that. It pays to shop around for the best price because they are often marked down, but don't buy just on price. There are poor wines among the *crus* too. Stick to the recommended producers unless someone you trust touts someone else.

Age: 1–3 years, some will hold longer in good
    vintages; Morgon and Moulin à Vent up to 5 or
    more
Price: $7.50–12 +
Recommended Producers: Jean Bédin, Georges
    Brun, Château de la Chaize (Brouilly), Joseph
    Drouhin, Georges Duboeuf ✪, Pierre Ferraud,
    Sylvain Fessy, Louis Jadot, Jacky Janodet ♦,
    Prosper Maufoux, Mommessin, Château Thivin,
    Trenel ♦
Foods: Chicken, sausages, liver and kidney, roast
    pork, goat cheese, semisoft cheeses, blues

Bourgogne Rouge

Made entirely from Pinot Noir, wines labeled Bourgogne Rouge can offer good value but are somewhat uneven. A lot more are produced than ever make it to the United States, among them some quite expensive. Good ones are like lesser Burgundies, with appealing Pinot Noir fruit, simple and forthright, with less tannin and body, though some Bourgogne can be rather gutsy. Poor ones can be thin, hard, and lacking in charm. Bourgogne Passe-tout-grains, more rarely seen, is a fruity blend of Pinot Noir and Gamay.

Age: 2–5 years
Price: $8–10 +
Recommended Producers: Chanson, De Courcel,
    Debord, André Delorme, Joseph Drouhin,
    Dubreuil-Fontaine, J. Faiveley, Goubard Mt.
    Avril, Jaffelin, Jayer-Gilles ✳, M. Juillot, Pierre
    Labet, Philippe Leclerc, Olivier Leflaive,
    Perrot-Minot Passe-tout-grains, Domaine
    Talmard, du Vieux St. Sorlin
Foods: Duck, coq au vin, liver and kidney, roast
    pork, veal, goat cheese

BURGUNDY (White)

While the great whites from the Côte d'Or are
beyond the scope of this book, there are excellent buys in wines from the Mâconnais region
and, very occasionally, the Côte Chalonnais
(Rully and Montagny). White wines from any
Burgundy appellation are made from Chardonnay, though Aligoté is a lesser white grape that
is also grown in parts of the region.

Chardonnay produces the greatest of the
world's dry white wines, and some of the most
expensive. But Chardonnay also performs at
lesser levels, yielding stylish, vibrant, and very
appealing wines that offer superb value. They
are wines that drink best in one to three years.
Their clean, crisp flavors, simpler and more neutral than the bigger, more expensive whites of
the Côte d'Or (Meursault, Chablis, the Montra-
chets), can handle a variety of foods.

Aligoté

Aligoté is a white grape that runs a distant second to Chardonnay in Burgundy. It is a dry, me-

dium-bodied white, fruity but fairly neutral in character. Traditionally it was the wine used in the popular aperitif Kir, which consists of a few drops of *crème de cassis* and dry white wine. Aligoté is still used for the Kir in Burgundy, though today the wine may well be Mâcon-Villages. Young, well-balanced Aligoté can be very pleasant, and a decent buy, and has recently become more widely available in the United States.

Age: 1–2 years
Price: $9–12
Recommended Producers: Boillot, Dubreuil-Fontaine, Faiveley La Paulée, Domaine Fichet, Louis Jadot, Jayer-Gilles, Louis Latour, Daniel Rion, M. Rollin, A&P Villaine ♦
Foods: Light fish, chicken, steamed vegetables; good aperitif, especially with cassis (Kir)

Bourgogne Blanc

Always Chardonnay and now often labeled as such. The wines can come from anywhere in Burgundy, so do not always show well-defined or distinctive character. From some producers, however, they are quite good, dry, and full-bodied, with the firm, slightly steely fruit of simple Burgundian Chardonnay. Aged briefly in oak, sometimes not at all. If you find it for $10–12 from a good producer, you get great value. Prices for Bourgogne Blanc have risen, however, and if you want to stay at $12 or less, check out discount stores, or look for Saint-Véran.

Age: 1–3 years, some will go for 4 or 5
Price: $8–12 +

Recommended Producers: Bachelet, B. Morey,
   Hubert Bouzereau, Chartron & Trebuchet ♦,
   Henri Clerc, Joseph Drouhin, Jean Germain,
   Michel Goubard, Louis Jadot, François Labet,
   Louis Latour, Olivier Leflaive, Rene Manvel,
   J. Moreau Chardonnay, Prieur-Brunet
Foods: Fish, chicken breast, shellfish; aperitif or Kir

Chablis

The best Chablis will always cost well above $12
a bottle, but there are several wines from the
simple appellation Chablis (as opposed to *grand
cru* or *premier cru*) available for less. French
Chablis, made entirely from Chardonnay, comes
from northern Burgundy, where the cooler climate produces crisp, dry wine with an appealing
mineral character—a classic with raw oysters.

Age: 1–3 years
Price: $10–12 +
Recommended Producers: Domaine Besson, E.
   Boileau, J-M Brocard, Alain Corcia, J. C.
   Dauvissat, Duplessis, Henri Laroche, Lupé-Cholet,
   Domaine de la Maladière, J. Moreau, Ropiteau,
   R. Vocoret
Foods: Oysters on the half shell, whitefish, shellfish,
   goat cheese

CÔTE CHALONNAISE

This region between Burgundy's Côte d'Or and
Mâcon produces a preponderance of red wines
made from Pinot Noir and somewhat fewer
whites, mostly Chardonnay but some Aligoté.

Less well known than other Burgundian appellations, they are often marked down. Look for stylish whites and reds with appellations such as Bouzereau, Givry, Mercurey, Montagny, and Rully (reds from superior vintages 1990, '92, '94).

Age: 1–3 years, 2–8 for reds
Price: $11–12
Recommended Producers: Caves de Buxy, Delaunay, André Delorme, Domaine Michel Goubard, Jafélin, M. Juillot, Louis Latour, Domaine Leflaive, Renarde, A&P Villaine
Foods: White: fish, shellfish, chicken breast; Red: duck, lamb, roast chicken, liver, sausage

---

Mâcon-Villages (also known as Mâcon Blanc, Mâcon Clessé, Mâcon Ige, Mâcon-Lugny, Mâcon-Viré)

The best-known and most widely available white Burgundy, from a large region of vineyards near the town of Mâcon, Pinot Noir and Gamay are also grown here, but the region is known mostly for Mâcon Blanc. Fresh, crisp, very dry, sometimes to the point of seeming austere, it is made entirely from Chardonnay. Most wines are not aged in oak, giving them a simple fruit character. Mâcon from good, reputable producers is an excellent value, and there are many, though numerous mediocre ones exist as well. Prices for some wines have inched beyond $10, but there are plenty of good buys for that or less.

Age: 1–2 years, can go 3
Price: $7–10 +
Recommended Producers: Daniel Barraud, André

Bonhomme, Joseph Drouhin, Georges Duboeuf ✪,
Andre Dupuis, Sylvain Fessy, Domaine Fichet,
Domaine de Greffière, Louis Jadot ✪, Louis
Latour, Cave des Lugny Les Charmes,
Manciat-Poncet, Prosper Maufoux, Michel
Nathan, Domaine Perrin, Domaine Prieulé,
Domaine des Roches, Domaine Talmard,
Domaine Thomas, Caves de Viré Le Grand
Cheneau

Foods: Simply prepared fish, shrimp, scallops,
chicken breast, cold roast chicken or turkey,
chicken salad, quiche; also a good aperitif, makes
an excellent Kir

Pouilly-Fuissé

Prices for this white Burgundy, made from Chardonnay, fluctuate considerably. A number of
decent ones fall within the $12 limit—and are
often overpriced when they're beyond that.
Some can even be found marked down for $9.99
or so. They are richer and more full-bodied than
Mâcon.

Age: 1–3 years
Price: $10–12 +
Recommended Producers: Jean-Claude Boisset,
Chanson, Georges Duboeuf ✪, Josselin, Jean
Jermain, Labouré-Roi, Henri Laroche, Gilles
Noblet, Ropiteau
Foods: Fish, shellfish, chicken, goat cheese

Saint-Véran ✪

This appellation, also in the Mâconnais region, is
a cut above Mâcon-Villages in character and
body and an excellent alternative to Pouilly-

Fuissé, many of which are now well beyond $10. Some Saint-Véran also cost a few dollars more, but excellent ones can be found for $10, sometimes less, especially at discount stores. Saint-Véran is often given a few months in oak, which gives it an extra degree of richness and complexity.

Age: 2–4 years
Price: $8–10
Recommended Producers: Jean-Claude Boisset, Alain Corcia, Georges Duboeuf ✪, Andre Dupuis, T. Guerin, Louis Jadot, Domaine Laroche, Cave de Lugny Les Monts, Prosper Maufoux, Michel Nathan, Les Trois Pêcheurs, J. J. Vincent
Foods: Richer fish preparations, shellfish, fish or chicken in cream sauce, seafood pastas, goat cheese

---

LANGUEDOC-ROUSILLON

This sprawling region in southern France, often referred to as the Midi, teems with vineyards that for years produced mostly plonk. Buckets of plonk are still produced here, but enterprising producers have replanted many vineyards to better varieties (Cabernet, Merlot, Syrah, Chardonnay) and have modernized production. Some very appealing red wines have begun to surface in parts of the Languedoc, particularly within appellations like Aude, Corbières, Costières de Nimes, Coteaux du Languedoc, Côtes de Rousillon, Faugeres, Gard, Minervois, and St. Chinian, as well as stylish nonappellation wines labeled Pays d'Oc. These include varietal wines labeled Cabernet Sauvignon, Merlot, Chardonnay and

Rhône grapes such as Syrah, Mourvèdre, and Cinsaut for reds, Viognier and Marsanne for whites.

Some of these wines have been so highly praised that prices have streaked well beyond $12. Some wines that seemed remarkable values when they were unknown and sold for $8 or $10 do not always seem a great value at $16 or $18. Some terrific values for $7 to $12 remain, however. Best buys within our price range are listed below, but it is worth noting that new properties are coming on line; so be on the lookout for new discoveries.

In terms of age, styles vary. A Corbières like Domaine de Fontsainte (see Corbières) is quite drinkable when you buy it, though substantial enough to age four or five years. A denser, more tannic red like Château du Campuget, however, needs a good two or three years to become so. Check it out with your wine merchant; if he knows enough to stock these wines, he should be able to advise you about drinkability.

Age: 2–8 years, depending on the wine
Price: $7–10
Recommended Producers: Domaine de l'Aigle, Gilbert Alquier, Château de Blomac, Domaine Capion ✪, Château du Campuget, Catherine de Saint-Juery, Domaine Clavel, Daniel Domergue, Domaine Dona Baisses, Château Donjon, Château des Estanille, Domaine de Fonsalade, Château de Gourgazaud, Château Hauterive, Domaine de l'Hortus, Château de Jau, Domaine Les Jouglas, Mas Jullien, Alain Jungenet, Domaine Laroque, Château Lascaux ✪, Château Miguel, Château Paraza, Château Ricardelle, Château Rouquette sur Mer, Reserve St. Martin, Sarda-Malet

---

Cahors

A sound, balanced red made mostly from Malbec blended with Tannat and Merlot or Cabernet Sauvignon. The region is east of Bordeaux, and the wines are somewhat similar but more rustic. The best have good structure, a good smack of tannin that allows them to age several years. Cahors is a terrific value—not a lot is available in the United States, but most of what does come in is from the better producers. As its popularity and value are recognized, prices are rising, but good ones can be had for $12 or less.

Age: 2–6 years, can go 8–10
Price: $8–12
Recommended Producers: Château Cascadais, Château de Chambert, Clos de Gamot ♦, Domaine de Haute-Serre, Moulin de la Grezette ✪, Château Pech de Jammes, Château de Peyros, Domaine de Quattre, La Tour de Vayrols, Clos Triguedina
Foods: Lamb, beef, veal, meat stews, mellow cheeses like Mimolette, Port Salut

---

Corbières

The region of Corbières has exploded in new or replanted vineyards in recent years. Rhône varieties like Syrah, Mourvèdre, Carignan, and Grenache produce some of the sturdiest, most attractive reds, such as Domaine de Fontsainte. Many of the same varieties are used for brisk, dry Corbières rosé. Some of the whites are also appealing, more so in fact than the majority of Rhône whites of similar price levels. The whites are usually blends of Grenache Blanc, Ugni Blanc, and Bourboulenc, with varying amounts of Chardonnay or Sauvignon Blanc. They are simple and dry but fresh when very young, and quite versatile with food. New labels are rapidly surfacing, and worth inquiring about from your wine merchant.

Age: 1–2 years for Corbières blanc and rosé, 2–4 for rouge, can hold for 5–8

Price: $6–12

Recommended Producers: Château Beauregard, Jean Berail, Château Capendu, Les Deux Rives, Etang des Colombes, Domaine de Fontsainte "Reserve la Demoiselle" ✪, Mas Champart, Saint Auriol, Domaine Serres Mazard, Clos Villemajou, La Voulte-Gasparets

Foods: Hearty meats and cheeses with reds; ham, smoked meats, and grilled vegetables with rosés; light fish, chicken, and pasta with whites

LOIRE VALLEY

The Loire Valley is a scant two hours by autoroute from Paris. The Loire River runs some six hundred miles from the center of France to the Atlantic. This picturesque region, with its historic châteaux, charming towns, and pastoral countryside, is home to several of France's best-known wines, including Muscadet, Sancerre, Chinon, and Vouvray. Most are white or rosé, except for Chinon, Bourgueil, and a soupçon of Sancerre Rouge.

The top appellations of Sancerre, Pouilly-Fumé, and Savennières, all dry whites, have escalated in price in recent years; there are a few exceptions noted. Muscadet, however, remains one of the great French wine values, especially in recent vintages, which have been very good to excellent. The wines of the Loire are treated alphabetically according to appellation.

Anjou

In this country most people think of sweetish rosés when they hear of the region Anjou. In fact, many of the best Anjou wines are dry whites, dry rosés, and supple red wines that nicely suit local cuisine. Anjou rouge, made from Cabernet Franc or Gamay, is a gently structured red that is best chilled, which makes it suitable for light meats, hearty pastas, or semisoft cheeses. Recommended: Domaine Baumard Logis de Giraudière, Domaine Cady, and Château La Tomaze, $8–10.

Rosés are made all over the Loire and are almost invariably dry but sweetened for export. Too bad. The dry ones are light-bodied, fruity, and refreshing, wonderful lunch and picnic wines when you are traveling through the Loire. Cabernet d'Anjou seems to have a little more dash and character than Rosé d'Anjou and is less cloyingly sweet. Recommended: Domaine de la Motte, Sauvion et Fils, $5–9.

Bourgueil

This is one of the better reds produced in the Loire, not very well known in the United States but very popular in Paris bistros and wine bars. Produced from Cabernet Franc, it has lively fruit hinting of berries and herbs. Good ones are soft and drinkable early, but some have the depth to age five or six years. Some of the best wines are labeled St. Nicholas de Bourgueil.

Age: 2–4 years, can go 5 or 6
Price: $8–10
Recommended Producers: Audebert, Domaine de la
    Chanteleuserie, Les Cloitres, Domaine du Grand
    Clos, Domaine Nicholas Jamet, Marcel Martin,
    Jacques Morin
Foods: Light meats and game birds, goat cheese

Chinon

Chinon and Bourgueil are often mentioned in the
same breath. Both are made from Cabernet
Franc, but Chinon is somewhat more vivid in
fruit and flavor—and generally more expensive.
Top producers like Joguet and Druet make impressive wines that can age a decade (they cost
$17 to $20). Lighter, decent Chinon can be
found, however, though once you've tasted a
flashier one, they may not satisfy. The lighter
ones benefit from light chilling. Try discount
shops where you may find Couly-Dutheil, for instance, for $10 or $11.

Age: 2–4 years, can do 5–8
Price: $9–12 +
Recommended Producers: B. Baudry, Marc Brédif,
    Domaine de la Chapelle, Domaine de la
    Chenetrie, Dozon, Marcel Martin, Jacques Morin,
    Olga Raffault, Sauvion
Foods: Cold meats, pâté campagne, roast chicken

Muscadet ✪

This crisp, snappy dry white offers terrific value.
It's a great summer wine, superb with fresh
oysters the rest of the year. It comes from the

region closest to the Atlantic, and is a versatile match with all sorts of seafood. The best Muscadet comes from the heart of the region known as Sèvre et Maine. The overall quality of Muscadet is higher than it used to be, a result of keen competition among the top producers. It is best consumed within two years of the vintage, when the fruit is fresh and sharp as an ocean breeze.

Age: 1–2 years, maybe 3
Price: $5–8
Recommended Producers: J. Aulanier, Barré
    Frères, A. Bregeon, Château du Cléray, Marquis
    de Goulaine, Domaine de l'Hyvernière, Marcel
    Martin, Louis Metaireau, Domaine de la Quilla,
    Château de la Rogotière, Clos de Rosiers, Sauvion
    et Fils ✪

Quincy

Barely known in the United States, this crisp white made from Sauvignon Blanc is a good alternative to the more expensive wines from this grape, Sancerre and Pouilly-Fumé. While it lacks their character and finesse, it is fresh, lively, and attractive.

Age: 1–2 years
Price: $12
Recommended Producers: Sauvion et Fils
Foods: Grilled or broiled fish, goat cheese

Sancerre

This distinctive white, made from Sauvignon Blanc, is one of my favorites from the Loire. Its crisp, tart fruit has its own *goût de terroir,* reminiscent of herbs, new-mown grass, and citrus with an appealing, mineral-like flavor. Scintillatingly dry, it is one of those wines that stir up the taste buds and whet the appetite. Prices, alas, have risen considerably as its popularity has increased. To find good Sancerre within our price limit, you'll have to search in discount stores or watch for specials.

Age: 2–3 years

Price: $9–10 + *(sales or specials)*

Recommended Producers: **Archambault Clos de la Perrière ♦, Clement-Cherrier, Comte Lafond, Cordier La Chaillou, Serge La Porte, Daniel Millet ♦, Andre Neveu, Henri Pelle, Domaine du Sarry, Sauterau, Sauvion, Château Thauvenay**

Foods: **Superb with goat cheese from the Loire; also fine with fish and seafood,** *boudin blanc,* **pâté**

Vouvray

Vouvray, made in the Touraine region from Chenin Blanc, is not easy to buy because you are rarely sure of what you are getting, especially at lower prices. Is it sweet or dry, or off-dry? If it is sweet, the label usually says Demi-sec. These can be wonderful wines and they last for years, but the finest are rare and expensive. Dry Vouvray is rarely labeled Sec—also rarely is it truly dry. When it is well balanced, a hint of sweetness adds richness and complexity and the wine is charming. Some Vouvrays, however, lack finesse and can be oversulphured.

Age: **2–4 years for Vouvray Sec, considerably longer for Demi-sec**

Price: $8–10 +

Recommended Producers: Marc Brédif, D.
   Champolou, Chapin-Landais, Duplessis-Mornay,
   Louis Duret, Kermit Lynch, Château de
   Moncontour, Château de Montfort, Clos Naudin,
   Prince Poniatowski ♦, Domaine Vaufuget

Foods: Dry Vouvray with smoked trout, *rillette,*
   liver, or country pâté, rabbit stew; Vouvray
   Demi-sec is a dessert wine, best on its own or
   with light cakes or cookies

PROVENCE

The south of France is churning. This large region stretches from the hills of Provence to the
Midi. Together the two regions produce the bulk
of France's so-called "country" wines and *vins
de table.* The new generation of winegrowers is
transforming this sprawling landscape, planting
new grape varieties (*cépages* in French), and establishing new quality standards. Many of the
reds have vivid fruit and vigorous, muscular
structure—rustic, spicy, earthy, and appealing.
The whites are less exciting, but cleaner,
fresher, zestier than they used to be; some are
quite charming, in fact.

Some of the most dynamic wines come from
Provence; many of the hot ones (Bandols such
as Domaine Tempier, Ott, Pibarnou) are well
beyond $12 a bottle. While in some instances the
steeper price tag is deserved, in others it is
highly presumptuous, particularly for whites and
rosés. Seekers of genuine value, however, such
as Kermit Lynch, Robert Kacher, and Dan Krav-
itz have turned up some rich and chewy little
marvels that are excellent value. These names

on a bottle mean the wine is always worth checking out.

Age: **Ready to drink, though some reds can age 4–8 years or more**
Price: **$8–12**
Recommended Producers: **Château Barbeyrolles, Commanderie de la Bargemone, Domaine Le Galantin, Domaine Gavoty, Les Jamelles, Château Maravenne, Mas de Cadenet Rouge and Blanc ✪, Mas de Gourgonnier ✪, Mas de la Rouvière, Mas Ste. Berthe, Château de Porcieux, Domaine Richeaume Rouge and Rosé, St.-Estève**

THE RHÔNE VALLEY

The Rhône Valley occupies a long, narrow corridor south of Lyons to Avignon. With vineyards situated either side of the Rhône River, the 120-mile valley produces some of France's greatest wines, especially grand, robust reds like Hermitage, Côte Rotie, and Châteauneuf-du-Pape—all of which are fairly grand in price too. Fortunately the Rhône also abounds in good, drinkable wines at moderate prices—Gigondas, Crozes-Hermitage, Vacqueyras. For casual occasions, or an everyday red, it's hard to beat good Côtes du Ventoux. These large appellations in the southern part of the Rhône make up more than 75 percent of total production, over 20 million cases annually. Most are quite ordinary, even mediocre, but exceedingly good ones exist if you know what to look for.

The best values in the Rhône are red. While the region makes very fine expensive whites (Condrieu, Hermitage Blanc, the sweet Muscat

Beaumes de Venise), the less expensive whites can be disappointing, coarse in flavor, and often lacking in freshness. The few exceptions are noted where appropriate. Tavel and other rosés are covered in the Rosé section (see).

Côtes-du-Rhône

The general appellation covers light-bodied, fruity reds made from several grape varieties grown in the southern Rhône as well as the noble red grape of the northern Rhône, Syrah. Good Côtes-du-Rhône has round, appealing, berryish fruit. The best ones, such as those from E. Guigal, Jaboulet, Domaine Ste.-Anne, and others are more intense, with peppery accents and very meaty flavors. Several such wines constitute Superbuys.

Age: 2–3 years, 4–6 for the best

Price: $6–9

Recommended Producers: Château d'Aigueville, A. Brunel, Domaine Brusset, Clos des Cazeaux, Domaines des Cedres, Michel Courtial, Domaine Santa Duc, Georges Duboeuf, Délas Frères, Domaine Durieu, Les Gouberts ☺, Domaine Gramenon, E. Guigal ☺, Jaboulet ☺, Kermit Lynch ☺, Domaines de Mont-Redon, Domaine St. Gayan, Château de Tours, Vidal-Fleury, Vieux Chênes

Foods: Highly versatile with casual foods, from hamburgers to barbecued meat, roast chicken, smoked turkey or duck, sausages, cheese and cheese dishes, goat cheese

---

Côtes du Ventoux

This is a lighter version of Côtes-du-Rhône, some-times too light to be much good. The exceptions, as noted, are punchier, with more fruit and style and can really be a super value, especially at discount stores, where they go for as little as $4.

Age: 1–3 years
Price: $5–8.50
Recommended Producers: Domaine des Anges, Domaine de Champaga, Chapoutier, Jaboulet, Château Pesquié, Vidal-Fleury, La Vieille Ferme Reserve ✪

Crozes-Hermitage

This sturdy red from the northern Rhône is made from Syrah grown in areas surrounding the great hill of Hermitage. It is similar to Hermitage, but smaller in scale and less complex—with one ex-ception, Jaboulet's Domaine de Thalabert, which in some vintages comes remarkably close to fine Hermitage. it has been "discovered" so is rarely, if ever, found for $12. Crozes-Hermitage can be thin and harsh in lesser vintages, though more consistent from the better producers.

Age: 3–5 years, the best can age well for 8–10 or longer
Price: $9–10 +
Recommended Producers: Michel Courtial, Délas Frères, Alain Graillot, Jaboulet, Domaine Pradelle, Domaine de Vallouit, Vidal-Fleury

Gigondas

This chewy, meaty red from the southern Rhône has become more popular in recent years. Some Gigondas is very intense and tannic in its early years, but mellows down with two to four years of aging. A few good ones can be found for $12 or less, others only on special or at discounters. Sturdy and robust, it's worth searching out.

Age: 3–5 years, can age
Price: $8–10 +
Recommended Producers: Clos des Cazeaux, Domaine du Gour de Chaule, Grand Montmirail ♦, E. Guigal, Jaboulet, Prosper Maufoux, Domaine Raspail, Château du Trignon ♦
Foods: Beef, game, meat stews, cassoulet, goat cheese

Vacqueyras

The vineyards near the town of Vacqueyras in the southern Rhône produce a somewhat meatier version of Côtes-du-Rhône and are entitled to use the appellation Côtes-du-Rhône-Villages. The fruit is more intense, the wines coarser and more tannic. Not necessarily a better buy than Côtes-du-Rhône, however, except as noted.

Age: 3–5 years
Price: $8–10
Recommended Producers: Clos des Cazeaux, Domaine de Couroulou, La Garrigue, Jaboulet
Foods: Meat stews, cassoulet, savory cheeses

Rhône

Other appellations are producing rich, muscular reds such as Cairanne and Lirac, while some (Côteaux du Tricastin, Sablet) produce more supple ones. Few of these appellations are well represented in the United States as yet, but they are beginning to see wider distribution. The Côtes du Lubéron borders Provence. Most producers make Rhône-style reds but fresh Provençal-like whites.

Age: 2–5 years
Price: $6–12
Recommended Producers: La Bouverie, Domaine Les Goubert Sablet Blanc ✪ and Rouge, Château de Mille (Luberon), Domaine La Rosière Syrah, Domaine de St. Luc, La Soumade Rasteau, Château du Trignon Sablet and Rasteau, Château Val de Joanis Rouge ✪ et Blanc (Côtes du Luberon)

THE SOUTHWEST

This area of France, the *sud/oest* as it is designated, is south of Bordeaux and encompasses Gascony and the Pyrenees. Appellations include Gaillac (red, white, and rosé), Madiran, a sturdy rustic red, and Cahors (see). The white wines are light, dry, and best quite young (such as the delightful Domaine de Pouy). Reds range from medium-bodied Gaillac and Côte de Gascogne to the darker, rugged Madiran, which traditionally accompanies cassoulet, the hearty meat-and-bean specialty of the region.

Age: 1–2 years for whites; 3–7 for reds, Madiran
   8–10

Price: $7.99–12 +

Recommended Producers: Château Bouscassé ✪,
   Château Colombière, Clos l'Eglise, Château
   Lestours, Domaine de Matibat, Château Pique
   Sigue, Domaine de Poujo, Domaine de Pouy ✪,
   Domaine La Salle, Domaine du Tariquet

Foods: White: aperitif, light fish; Red: meat, stews,
   savory cheese

ROSÉS

France produces tremendous quantities of rosé
wines, most dry, some sweet. A lot of it is quite
mediocre, including much of the well-known
sweet rosés from the Loire Valley labeled Rosé
d'Anjou, and even some interpretations of the
country's best-known rosé, Tavel. Tavel has long
been considered France's best rosé, but this is
no longer true. Today it stands in the shadow of
livelier, more vibrant rosés like Joguet's Chinon
Rosé, the Languedoc's rosé de Syrah, and the dry
rosés of Burgundy. These are sometimes labeled
vin gris—gris actually translates as "gray" but
really means a pale coral or flesh color. Since
there is so much variation in quality, the rosés
recommended here are from various parts of
France—the name of the producer is more important than the region. Some of the currently
touted rosés, especially those from recently discovered properties in Provence, have leaped to
what I consider unconscionable prices. Eighteen
dollars for a simple dry rosé? Come on, that's for
the "let-them-eat-cake" crowd. There are equally
good ones for considerably less.

Age: 1–2 years

Price: $6–10 +

Recommended Producers: Château d'Aqueria Tavel, la Bargemone, Château Beaupré Minervois, G. Bertrand Gris de Gris, Domaine Bruno Clair Marsannay, Georges Duboeuf Beaujolais, Fontsainte Gris de Gris, Domaine de l'Hortus, Les Jamelles, Domaine Lafond, Château Maravenne, Mas Champart ✪, Mas Julien Minervois, Mas Ste.-Berthe Les Baux, Domaine de la Morderée Tavel, Domaine La Moutète, Château Routas Rouvière, Château St. Roch, Sauvion d'Anjou, A. de Villaine Bourgogne ♦

VARIETAL WINES

Except for Alsace, French wines with distinctive character, whether expensive or modest in price, are usually labeled with regional or vineyard names. New development in several regions —such as the Haut-Poitou of the Loire, Provence, Languedoc-Rousillon, and several districts in Bordeaux—has resulted in what is building into a category all its own: varietals. These are wines made predominantly from a single grape variety, which appears on the label. Those most frequently seen are Chardonnay and Sauvignon Blanc for white wines, Cabernet Sauvignon and Merlot for reds. Some of the most popular wines are from the so-called Mediterranean varieties— Mourvèdre, Syrah, Cinsaut, and Grenache for reds, Viognier and Marsanne for whites. This category is growing fast.

The new varietals are not to be confused with regional varietals like the Bourgogne Blanc

(Chardonnay) and Rouge (Pinot Noir), which have something of the distinctive character of their region. The newer wines are rather neutral in most cases, the best of them clean, well balanced, tasting of the grape that produces them. As yet, there are not a great many to recommend, and the good from the mediocre are still in the process of sorting themselves out. It is definitely a category to watch.

Age: 1–2 years for whites; 2–4 for reds
Price: $4.50–8
Recommended Producers: Domaine des Acacias Sauvignon, Baron Briare (Sauvignon Blanc), Barton & Guestier, Joseph Drouhin, Georges Duboeuf, Fortant, Les Jamelles, Louis Jadot, Louis Latour, Domaine de Montmarin, J. Moreau, Christian Moueix (Merlot), J. & P. Moueix, Place d'Argent, Domaine Ravel, Regnard, Domaine Richeaume, Domaine de Rivoire, Domaine La Rosière, Domaine La Source-Herault, Domaine de La Tuilerie, Val d'Orbieu

SUPERBUYS / FRANCE

Whites

Pinot Blanc, Alsace (Trimbach, Josmeyer, Beyer) $7–9
Château Bonnet, Bordeaux, $7.75
Domaine de Pouy, $6.99
Maître d'Estournel, Bordeaux, $6.99
Georges Duboeuf Mâcon-Village, Burgundy, $7.99
Mâcon-Lugny, Les Charmes, Burgundy, $7–8
Reserve St. Martin Viognier, $6.99
Sauvion et Fils Muscadet, $6–7
Les Goubert Sablet Blanc, Rhône, $7.99

Reds

Château de Belcier, Bordeaux, $7

Château Larose Trintaudon, Bordeaux, $8.99

Michel Lynch Rouge, Bordeaux, $5.99–7

Georges Duboeuf Beaujolais (Nouveau, Villages, Regnié), $6–9

Château du Campuget, Languedoc, $7.99–8.99

Domaine de Fontsainte, Corbières, $8.99

Château Greysac, Bordeau, $8.95

Château Lascaux, Provence, $10

Mas de Gourgonnier, Provence, $7.50

Jaboulet La Table du Roy, Rhône, $6

Côte-du-Rhône Rouge (Domaine Ste.-Anne, Guigal, Jaboulet, $6–8.99)

La Vieille Ferme Reserve, Rhône, $7.50–8.99

Château Val de Joanis Rouge, Rhône red, $8.99

Moulin de la Grezette, Cahors, $9–11

Rosés

Château Rouquette Sur Mer, $8.99

Mas Champart, $8.75

Reserve St. Martin Rosé de Syrah, $5.99

Les Jamelles Cinsaut Rosé, $6.99

Italy

Italy is a brimming vat of wine, the world's largest producer. There are nearly 2 million vineyards in Italy producing over 7 million liters of wine. Only some 13.5 percent of it, however, comes under the appellation laws known as *Denominazione d'origine controllata* (DOC), which comprises most of what we import to this country—in other words, we get the best.

American wine consumers used to Italian wine bargains—remember the days of $9 Barolo (*good* ones!), $7 Chianti Riserva, and $4 Pinot Grigio? —are having a rough time adjusting to double-digit prices. Those days are gone; prices for each of those wines have doubled, even tripled. One can take solace in the fact, however, that the increased global demand for good wine has forced Italian winemakers into a greater commitment to quality. This can be seen not only with the new, innovative wines that began to appear in the eighties but with traditional types as well. Orvieto, for example, a rather ordinary, often mediocre white wine from the hill town of Umbria, has never been better than today—fresh, crisp, dry—all one could want in a simple, inexpensive white wine for everyday or casual occasions.

The DOC laws cover nearly five hundred different styles of Italian wine. Instituted in 1963, DOC aimed to raise standards for winegrowing all over Italy and bring the wines into the main arena of international recognition. If the DOC designation on a wine is somewhat less important now, it is because the law has done its work over the past two decades to give Italian winemakers a common aim: making quality wines and seeing it pay off. Today, however, many in the wine trade consider the system controversial and confusing to consumers. Some of the country's best wines, for instance, are proprietary blends like Tignanello, Sammarco, La Pergola Torte, Montesodi, and dozens of other expensive wines that initially won international acclaim without such designation.

For our purposes here, with our $12-a-bottle limit, we must stick to the affordable best. The list necessarily excludes some of Italy's most famous wine names, like Barolo, Barbaresco, Brunello di Montalcino, Taurasi, Arneis, and the growing host of proprietary wines like those mentioned above—they cost well upward of $15 a bottle.

Fortunately there is enough good, flavorful wine at more modest prices that those who want to enjoy Italian wines for everyday or casual occasions needn't suffer. You have to know the right producers, though. There are probably twenty-five or more Pinot Grigios available in the

United States; quality varies considerably, and perhaps a dozen are worth the price—you can get burned with lousy wines or by overpaying. It's wise to stick to the names recommended here, unless your wine merchant has discovered a "find" that he personally recommends.

WHITE WINES

Italy has long been known for exceptional red wines, but whites, for the most part, were traditionally modest and simple at best, bobbing along in oceans of quite ordinary, even mediocre, wines. Italy's top whites, like Gavi di Gavi, Fiano di Avellino, and Arneis, can be intriguing and quite good, but they are often very expensive. In fact, restaurant wine lists account for most of their sales in this country.

Trebbiano is the most widely grown white variety, producing most of the white wines of central Italy (Toscano Bianco, Galestro of Tuscany, Orvieto and Torgiano of Umbria, Frascati and Trebbiano di Aprilia of Latium). Some of these are rather fragile wines, often better on the spot than when they arrive on these shores. Varietal wines are hugely on the increase: Chardonnay, Sauvignon, Pinot Bianco, Tocai. Quality varies tremendously; it's best to avoid the cheapest (under $5).

Bianco di Custoza

A clean dry white from the Veneto, southwest of Verona, very similar in fruit character (blended from the same white grapes) to Soave, sometimes superior. Limited distribution.

Age: 12–18 months
Price: $6–7
Recommended Producers: La Columbaia, Lamberti,
   Santa Sofia, Tommasi, Zenato
Foods: Shellfish, boiled or grilled, seafood pasta,
   risotto

Bianco di Toscana (Tuscan Whites)

Trebbiano was traditionally the grape used for
Tuscan whites that were mild in flavor and character. Quality producers, however, have reduced
yields to get more fruit intensity (as in Coltibuono Bianco) or added better grapes such as Pinot
Bianco, Sauvignon Blanc, and Chardonnay to the
blend. Good ones have appealing fruit and bracing acidity that make them excellent food wines.

Age: 1–2 years
Price: $7–10
Recommended Producers: Altesino, Antinori,
   Avignonesi, Badia a Coltibuono ✪, Barbi, Brolio,
   Castellare, Castello di Volapai, Le Crette Val
   d'Arbia, Diévole, Frescobaldi, Gabbiano, Podere
   Il Palazzino, Terre Toscane, Trappoline ✪
Foods: Antipasti; seafood pastas, pasta primavera,
   pasta with mushrooms; fish and shellfish; white
   meat chicken; prosciutto

Breganze di Breganze

This unusual proprietary white is one of the best
values from Fausto Maculan, a top producer in
the Veneto. Crisp, dry, lively citrus flavors make
it versatile with food. Chardonnay gives it character.

Age: 1–2 years
Price: $12 +
Sole Producer: Fausto Maculan

Chardonnay

Chardonnay on the label is a guaranteed sale
these days, no matter what the price tag. Italian
Chardonnay remains one of the bargain whites
in Italy in the $8–10 range. Cheaper ones are
mostly from large producers whose wines have
little character and therefore are *not* good buys.
The better ones are dry, medium-bodied, with
brisk fruit flavors. They get little or no oak aging
and are quite versatile with food, more so than
weightier Chardonnays, which can be overpowering for all but the richest dishes. Don't be
shocked to find increasingly expensive Chardonnays coming out of Italy, especially oak-aged versions from Tuscany, Umbria, and the Piedmont.
These wines, aiming at styles similar to white
Burgundy and California Chardonnay, are a different breed and expensive (*and,* might I add,
sometimes overpriced!).

Age: Best at 1–2 years but may go 3 or 4 from
    superior vintages like 1994
Price: $7–12
Recommended Producers: Batasiolo ♦, Boscaini, J.
    Brigl, La Cadalora, Il Cardo, Castelcosa, Castello
    di Ama, Collavini, Enofriulia, Fratelli Pighin,
    Kettmeir, Lageder, Leone de Castris, di Lozzolo,
    Lungarotti, Maso Poli, Midolini, Nozzole Le
    Brunicche, Pecorari, Pierpaolo, Pio Cesare,
    Plozner ✪, Pravis, Ruffino Libaio ✪, San Felice,
    Santa Margherita ♦, J. Tiefenbrunner ✪,
    Tommasi, Valdo, Villanova, Peter Zemmer

Foods: **Seafood pastas, risotto, shellfish, chicken breast, rabbit; also a serviceable aperitif**

Frascati

Mostly light and nondescript, but dry and sometimes attractively fruity, especially those labeled *Superiore*. Not strongly recommended since other Italian whites offer better value.

Age: **1–2 years**
Price: **$5–8**
Recommended Producers: **Colli di Catone, Colli di Tuscolo, Fontana Candida, Monteporzio, Pallavicini, San Marco, Villa Masseto, Villa Simone**
Foods: **Antipasti, seafood salads, especially mussels**

Galestro

Made from the white grapes of the Chianti region (Trebbiano, Pinot Bianco, Malvasia), this brisk, light-bodied wine is also light on flavor, too much so much of the time, and it can be bitingly crisp. The better ones have a lively zest that is appealing. The fruit does not hold much beyond the first year, so beware of anything older.

Age: **8–12 months**
Price: **$6–8**
Recommended Producers: **Antinori, Cecchi, Frescobaldi, Gabbiano, Rocca della Macie, Ruffino, San Felice**
Foods: **Antipasti; also makes a good wine spritzer**

Gavi

The Piedmont's best-known white wine, made from the Cortese di Gavi grape. Well-made Gavi is dry and medium-bodied, with lively fruit and fresh aromas; the fruit is fairly delicate in young wines, but flavors deepen after a couple of years in the bottle. Considered one of the top Italian whites for fish and seafood, but prices for the best ones have jumped to $15 and more; good ones are still available for less.

Age: 1–2 years, though some will age nicely for 2–3
Price: $8.50–10 +
Recommended Producers: Abbona la Marchesa, Bolla, Cada Meo, Foro, Fausto Ghemme, La Guardia, Marchesi di Barolo, Massone, Monfrino, Oddero, Palladino, Rocca Caselli, La Scolca ✪, Tassarolo 'S,' Villa Banfi Principessa, Villa Rosa
Foods: Fish and seafood dishes, pasta with white truffles

Lacryma Christi del Vesuvio

Produced on the volcanic slopes of Vesuvius, Lacryma Christi (whose name means "tears of Christ") has long been a popular wine in and around Naples. It is simple dry white with no pretensions, but the leading estate in the region, Mastroberardino, makes something more of it than that in a crisp, attractive version. The red is also good, agreeably earthy.

Age: 1–2 years
Price: $10 +
Recommended Producers: Grotta del Sole, Mastroberardino ♦, Saviano

Foods: Pasta with squid, mussels, or marinara
  sauce; chicken cacciatore

Lugana

A delicate white from Lombardy from a DOC
region that extends into the Veneto. Not widely
available in the United States, light-bodied Lugana can be fresh and charming from good producers but is sometimes dull and lacking in flavor
by the time it gets here. It's at its best locally.

Age: 1 year; good ones gain in flavor up to 2 or 3
Price: $7–9
Recommended Producers: Boscaini, Lamberti,
  Provenza, Santi ✪, Zenato
Foods: Pasta primavera, delicate fish; drinks well on
  its own

Müller-Thurgau

This white, from a grape that is a cross between
Riesling and Sylvaner, is not for everyone. Young
wines are dry to the point of being austere, but
in good ones the steeliness softens with a year or
so in the bottle, and the wine is attractive with
simply prepared fish.

Age: Best at 2–3 years
Price: $6.50–10 +
Recommended Producers: Enofriulia, Kettmeir ✳,
  Pojer & Sandri
Foods: Trout, sole, herb-flavored goat cheese

Orvieto

This Umbrian white, traditionally made in dry
(*secco*) and sweet (*abboccato*) styles, had degen-

erated into very ordinary stuff until producers like Antinori, Ruffino, and a few others began upgrading quality in the late eighties. Today, Orvieto is one of the best values in Italian whites. Mediocre wines are still made, however, so stick to the producers recommended below. Orvieto is dry, but not severely so like some of the wines of the northeast. The fruit is round and appealing with crisp acidity, and the wines are best when quite young and fresh.

Age: 1–1½ years
Price: $6.50–9
Recommended Producers: Antinori Campogrande ✿, Barbi, Melini, Palazzone, Rocca della Macie, Ruffino ✿, Il Tasso, Vaselli, LeVelette
Foods: Pastas with cream sauce, fish and seafood, rabbit, salads with light vinaigrette

Pinot Bianco

The Pinot Bianco grape is widely grown in northern Italy and results in wines ranging from ordinary to quite stylish and fragrant, depending on the producer. Some of the best come from regions of Friuli and go for considerably more than $12 a bottle; good ones exist for less, but avoid the very cheap ones, which are poor value. In Tuscany the grape may be blended with Chardonnay with excellent results.

Age: 1–2 years
Price: $8–12
Recommended Producers: Antinori Bianco Toscana, La Cadalora, Enofriulia, Lageder, Volpe Pasini, Maso Poli, Schwanberg, Terlano, Tiefenbrunner
Foods: Seafood pastas (but not too spicy), sole and

similar fish, fettucine Alfredo, chicken with
cream sauce

Pinot Grigio

One of the most popular whites from Italy, now
widely available in the United States. Quite dry,
with zesty fruit and piquant flavors in the best
wines, but mediocre ones—on the increase due
to demand—are thin and lack flavor. Produced
mainly in the northeast regions of Alto-Adige
(where acidity is highest), Trentino, Friuli, and
the Veneto. Prices have risen for the better ones,
but those over $12 are rarely worth it. Excep-
tions: Livio Felluga ($15), Abbazia di Rosazzo
($16.50), Jermann.

Age: 1–2 years, superior vintages
Price: $7–10 +
Recommended Producers: Duca Badoglio, Bollini,
   Boscaini, Cadalora Valagarini, Casal del Ronco,
   Cavit, Collavini, La Colombaia, Enofriulia, Barone
   Fini, Furlan, Kettmeir, Lageder, Lungarotti, I
   Mesi, Pecorari, Pravis, Doro Princic, San
   Valentino ✪, Santi, Tiefenbrunner, Tommasi,
   Valdo, Valfieri, Villa del Borgo, Peter Zemmer
Foods: Seafood, especially shellfish (steamed
   mussels, clams), pastas with garlic and oil, *pesto*
   sauce, goat cheese, grilled eggplant

Pomino Bianco

Though made only by Frescobaldi, Pomino has
its own DOC appellation in the Chianti Rufina
region of Tuscany. This wine, a balanced white
blend of Trebbiano, Pinot Bianco, and Chardon-

nay, used to be better until Frescobaldi siphoned off the best lots for the reserve style "Il Benefizio" ($24), which also contains Chardonnay. It's still a quite decent dry white, however.

Age: 1–3 years
Price: $8–11
Recommended Producers: Frescobaldi
Foods: Antipasti, fettucine Alfredo, and light pastas, simple fish and chicken dishes

Sauvignon

Italian Sauvignon Blanc has a crisp, lively fruit that is tart when very young but softens with a year or so in bottle. Most have sharp acidity and grassy aromas that best suit slightly acidic foods; they may, in fact, be too tart for some palates. Top producers in Friuli and the Veneto get well over $12 for their Sauvignons; some are worth it, but many are overpriced.

Other regions, such as Tuscany and Umbria, are starting to experiment with the Sauvignon grape.

Age: 1–2 years, occasionally 3
Price: $8–11
Recommended Producers: Antinori Borro della Salla ♦, Collio, Conti d'Attimis, Enofriulia, Furlan, Lageder, Midolini, Schwanberg, Tiefenbrunner, Villa del Borgo, Villa Volpe
Foods: Seafood and seafood pastas, goat cheese (including salads and pizzas)

Soave

Can all the wines labeled Soave really be from Soave? Possibly, since the area surrounding the town is choked with vines, but it's questionable. High yields account for the wine's abundance, but it rarely offers more than reasonably clean but neutral flavors, and some are wretched. Bolla is decent and consistent. The best Soave is Soave Classico and Classico Superiore, which cost more but are worth it since they have a bit more character. Only those appellations are recommended here.

Age: 1–2 years, may go 3
Price: $7–10
Recommended Producers: Anselmi ✪, Bisson, Bolla, Boscaini, R. Farina, Gini, Guerrieri-Riccardi, Masi, Pieropan, Luigi Righetti, Santa Sofia, Santi, Tommasi, Zenato
Foods: Light pastas (seafood, cream sauce, primavera, etc.), fish and seafood, chicken breast

Tocai

In the Veneto and especially Friuli, Tocai is the favorite white, but it is not well known in the United States. Its distinctive scent, a mingle of wildflowers, dried grasses, and hints of almond, is intriguing, with appealing fruit that is lively and fresh but surprisingly full-bodied. The good ones get better with bottle age, and those from producers like Jermann and Livio Felluga become quite complex. Tocai deserves to be better known here, but it may take a while, as it is something of an acquired taste.

Age: 1–2 years, may well go 3 to 4
Price: $8–10 +
Recommended Producers: Collavini, Conti d'Attimis, Enofriulia, Marco Felluga, Plozner, Doro Princic,

Sant'Elena de Gradisco, Santa Margherita,
Zenato
Foods: Fish and shellfish, Oriental fish and chicken
dishes, spicy pilaf

Torre di Giano

This dry white from the region of Umbria is a
firm, medium-bodied dry wine made from Trebbiano; good value.

Age: 1–2 years
Price: $7–9
Recommended Producers: Lungarotti
Foods: Fish, chicken, seafood, pasta

Verdicchio

Another popular white that has grown blander
due to excessive demand. Good ones, however,
have that brisk, racy fruit that snaps with crisp-
ness. Best when quite young and fresh.

Age: 9–18 months
Price: $7.50–10
Recommended Producers: Bischi, Bucci, Colonnara,
   Fazi-Battaglia, Garofoli Macrina, Monte Schiavo
Foods: Fish and shellfish

Vernaccia di San Gimignano

Vernaccia has become one of Italy's hottest
whites in recent years, and is interesting because
it has a rather unusual almond character and
can be faintly bitter in aftertaste. Good ones are

smooth and round, with lively fruit and flavors that often become more complex with a couple of years in bottle. Part of its charm derives, no doubt, from the picturesque town of San Gimignano that most American tourists visit when they go to Tuscany. Cheaper versions are often bland and lacking in flavor.

Age: 1–3 years

Price: $6–10

Recommended Producers: Il Cipressino, Riccardo Falchini, Giannina, Pietrafitta, Rocca della Macie, Monte Molini, Montenidolo, San Quirico, Savestro, Strozzi, Teruzzi e Puthod ✪, Angelo del Tufo

Foods: Gnocchi with porcini mushrooms, sole amandine, fish, broiled or poached with light sauce

---

REDS

Good buys abound in Italian reds; there are some real knockouts. Italy makes its share of light, insipid reds (like Bardolino, for instance), but most Italians prefer chewy reds—Barbera, Dolcetto, Rosso di Montalcino, Salice Salentino —with big, meaty flavors that are wonderful to drink.

These wines are lesser in stature but not necessarily in weight or concentration. To take an example: Barolo and Barbaresco are the lords of the Piedmont region, but their prices are well above our $12 ceiling. Barbera d'Alba (as well as its fraternal twin, Barbera d'Asti) and Dolcetto are the everyday reds in the Piedmont. Actually, they used to be less expensive than they are today, but they've been "discovered." Barberas used to go for $9 a bottle, now they're $10 to $12, well above that from some estates. The same is true for Rosso di Montalcino, a red that has zoomed in popularity, and prices are inching upward with each vintage. Some of the increases are due to the exchange rate, though not all. When the dollar bounces back, as it eventually will, prices will stabilize somewhat.

Chianti has gone up too, but so has quality for many Chianti estates. Chianti made its fame as a cheap ($1.50, $1.99 once upon a time) fruity red bottled in straw-covered flasks, and it has had a hard time breaking away from that image. Consumers who knew the good wines had the advantage for years because the better wines just couldn't command high prices. The DOC laws themselves hampered upgrading the wines, requiring that the blend for Chianti include the local white varieties, Trebbiano and Malvasia. Once the laws were changed, higher standards favored the better producers, and prices have risen, steeply in some cases.

Happily there are still good Chiantis to be had for $12 or less, even if not as many. And it's a good idea to look out for price cuts on the expensive ones, though they are rarer than before.

Some of the best buys are simple *rossos* (*rosso* is Italian for red), which can be regional wines like Rosso di Montalcino or Rosso Cónero, made by several producers; sometimes they are individual brands, such as Coltibuono Rosso, Rosso della Quercia, or Corvo, and have their own entry as such.

Barco Real

A somewhat lighter but appealing version of Car-
mignano ($15–20) from Tuscany, and thus simi-
lar to Chianti; often beefier; increasingly made,
very good value.

Age: 2–3 years
Price: $10–12
Sole Producer: Cappezzana
Foods: Roast chicken, grilled meat, lasagne and
   other meat pastas, pizza

Barbera d'Alba
Barbera d'Asti
Barbera del Monferrato

Barbera d'Alba has the largest production and is
the richest of the three, a fruity, chewy red that
is generally drinkable in its second or third year
(tannic ones may need longer). If well balanced,
they age nicely six to eight years and are excellent value to buy in quantity. Barbera d'Asti is
lighter in density and body, with vivid fruit, also
good value. Neither is to be confused with Barbera del Monferrato, which is lighter still and
sometimes a bit fizzy *(frizzante)*.

Age: 2–3 years, more concentrated ones age 6–8
Price: $7.50–10
Recommended Producers: Abbona, Anselma,
   Batasiolo, Castello di Neive ♦, Cavallotto, Clerico
   ♦, Contratto, G. Cortese, Dessilani, Farino,
   Fontanafredda, Marchesi di Barolo, Moccagatta,
   Oddero, Palladino, Prunotto, Punset, Renato
   Ratti, Rocche Costamagna, Valentino
Foods: Roast meats and poultry, pizza, meat pastas,

sausage and peppers, savory cheeses (Asiago, Bel
Paese, Cheddars)

Cabernet

Cabernet Sauvignon is now grown in many parts
of Italy and is frequently very expensive, made
in styles that stand with the best of California
and Bordeaux. The lighter Cabernets of the
northeast (Friuli, Trentino, Veneto) were until
recently made mostly from Cabernet Franc, but
lately they are increasingly blended with Cabernet Sauvignon or Merlot—and the better for
it. Cabernet Franc alone can be quite light and
somewhat thin. There are several DOC zones for
Cabernet in Friuli, Trentino, and the Veneto.
The lightest wines rarely compete with moderate-priced Cabernets from California, Chile, Bulgaria, but a few can and more have emerged in
recent years.

Age: 2–3 years, occasionally more
Price: $7.50–12
Recommended Producers: Bollini, Casal del Ronco,
   Cavit Riserva, Col di Sassa, Concilio Riserva,
   Marco Felluga, Plozner, Pravis, Sant'Elena di
   Gradisco, Santa Margherita, Schwanberg,
   J. Tiefenbrunner, Valdo, Gianni Vescovo,
   Villa Poggiolo
Foods: Roast pork, pasta with wild mushrooms,
   meat-sauce pastas

Chianti

When the region of Chianti in Tuscany decided
to upgrade quality, it moved to the highest offi-

cial category of Italian wines, DOCG (*Denominazione di origine controllata e guarantita*—name and origin controlled and guaranteed). Grape yields were lowered under the new rules, and the wines must now be tasted by a panel to qualify as Chianti. The result reduced quantities of Chianti by nearly half. Sangiovese remains the predominant grape for Chianti. Requirements for using white grapes went from 10 percent to 2 percent and permit up to 10 percent of other varieties, including Cabernet Sauvignon, which increases flavor intensity. Quality has jumped, especially for Riservas (better lots of wines that must be aged at least three years before release), but they are also much more expensive. Riservas from small, sought-after estates go for $14 to $26 a bottle, sometimes higher; some Riservas (Monte Vertine, Fontodi, Felsina Berardenga, Ruffino Gold Label, Querceto, Volpaia) can be worth it. Regular Chianti is a moderately light red, still uneven in quality but quite charming from the top producers. Those listed are consistently good; asterisks denote producers whose Riservas are sometimes discounted and therefore excellent value.

Age: 2–4 years; Riservas 4–6, and can go 8 or more
Price: $7–12
Recommended Producers: Antinori ✳, Aziano (Ruffino), Badia a Coltibuono Cetamrua, Brolio Riserva, Calcinaia, Castello di Ama, Castello di Gabbiano, Castello di Volpaia, Le Corti, Diévole, Felsina ❂, Fossi, Frescobaldi (Nipozzano), Isole e Olena, Lilliano, Luiano Montegrossi, Lucignano, Melini, Il Palazzino, Riserva Ducale, Rocca della Macie ✳, Ruffino, San Felice, San Giusto, San Ripolo, Verrazano, Villa Banfi ✳, Villa Cafaggio ✳, di Viticcio ✳

Foods: Pizza, hearty pastas with meat sauce,
   mushrooms, sausage, liver; Riservas with roast or
   grilled chicken, steak, game birds, sausage and
   peppers, veal chops

Coltibuono Rosso ✪

An excellent red from Badia a Coltibuono, one
of the top Chianti estates near Siena. Blended
from the Chianti red grapes, Sangiovese and Canaiolo Nero, with a small percentage of Cabernet
Sauvignon, this sturdy red is a Superbuy.

Age: 3 years, will age 4–6
Price: $8–10
Producer: Badia a Coltibuono
Foods: A versatile red, good with pizza, grilled beef,
   or chicken, other hearty fare

Corvo Rosso

This widely available Sicilian red is consistently
agreeable, normally not a qualification sufficient
to be included in this book. However, in superior
vintages like 1989 and 1994, it proved an exceptional value and is therefore worth considering.
(The Bianco is a commercially acceptable white
but nothing special.)

Age: 1–3 years
Price: $5–7
Producer: Duca di Salparuta
Foods: Braised chicken or veal, meatballs, lasagne,
   pizza

Dolcetto

The role of Dolcetto in the Piedmont, whose capital is Milano, is often likened to that of Beaujolais in France. Like Beaujolais, it is a quaffing wine, but much meatier. Dolcetto d'Acqui is lighter and not generally recommended; Dolcettos from Alba and Dogliani are the best. It is unfortunate that Dolcettos from some estates have shot beyond our price limit. Buy these with care. Dolcetto's appeal is its early thrust of flashy, berrylike fruit that balances tannin and acidity. Within two years, however, the cherubic fruit begins to fade and takes with it the young wine's charm. Catch it before the tannins and acid take over.

Age: 1–2 years, maybe 3 in exceptional vintages
Price: $9–12
Recommended Producers: Abbazia di Chiara, Abbona Papa Celso, Azelia, Batasiolo, Ca'de Monte, Castello di Neive ♦, Cavallotto, D. Clerico ✳, Contratto, Corino, Dezzani, Fantino, del Glicine, Elio Grasso, La Guardia, Manzone, Marcarini ✳, Marchese di Barolo, Martinenga, Mascarello, Moccagatta, Oddero, Palladino, A. Parusso, Pio Cesare, Punset, Renato Ratti, Bruno Rocca, Rocche Costamagna, Gigi Rosso, Terre del Dolcetto, Valfieri
Foods: Meat antipasti, cold smoked chicken or turkey, pizza, young savory cheeses like Ricotta Salata, Caprini, Dolcelatte

Gattinara

Made from the same grape, Nebbiolo, that produces Barolo, Gattinara is a mild-mannered version of medium body. Quality varies among producers in the region, and sometimes the wines are thin. Good ones, however, are well balanced and flavorful, and can age surprisingly well. Prices have risen considerably in recent years; more expensive ones (♦) are occasionally found on sale.

Age: Drinkable at 3–4 years, can hold to 8, 10, or more
Price: $8–10
Recommended Producers: Antoniolo, Bianchi, L&I Nervi ♦, Travaglini, Vallana ✪
Foods: Roast or grilled meat and poultry, veal scallopini, pasta or risotto with white truffles

Ghemme

A firm red from the Gattinara district of the Piedmont, also made from Nebbiolo and often a better value. Production is smaller, however, and it is not widely available.

Age: 4–8 years
Price: $9
Recommended Producers: Bianchi, Brugo, Le Colline, Oberto, di Sizzano, Troglia
Foods: Grilled steak, roast kid, lamb, *ossobuco*

Grumello (see Valtellina)

Inferno (see Valtellina)

Merlot

Merlot is widely grown in Italy, but many of the wines are light and grapey, lacking the plummy fruit character so attractive in good Merlot. There are many more good ones than previously, including those that are richer in style, which are often priced above $12 but occasionally found for less (as noted by the diamond below). Those from Colli Orientali and Colli Goriziano Grave in Friuli are among the best, especially Riservas.

Age: 2–4 years
Price: $8–10
Recommended Producers: Bollini, Casal del Ronco, Collavini, Marco Felluga, Franco Furlan, Gonzaga, Guerrieri, Lageder, Midolini, Plozner, Doro Princic ♦, Pietro Rubini, Santa Margherita, Torre di Luna, Luigi Valle
Foods: Rabbit, pork; lamb with Riservas

Monte Antico ✪

Superbuy red from the hills near Montalcino in Tuscany, made from Sangiovese and Canaiolo. Sturdy, rich but well balanced, it ages with some elegance and is superior to some Chianti Riserva.

Age: 3–4 years, will age 6–7
Price: $8–9

Recommended Producer: Castello di Monte Antico
Foods: Beef, lamb, hearty pastas, game birds

Montefalco Rosso

Firm, appealing red from Umbria, near the town
of Montefalco. Best is Rosso d'Arquata, blended
from Barbera, Canaiolo, and Merlot, and aged
in small oak; attractively robust but little known
outside the region. Sagrantino, another red from
the same area, is riper, more robust, less re-
fined, and sometimes sweet *(passito)*.

Age: Drinkable at 2–3 years, will age 4–6
Price: $7.50–10
Recommended Producers: Adanti, Antonello
Foods: Pastas with meat sauce, roast chicken, game
  birds

Montepulciano d'Abruzzi Rosso

Wines from the Abruzzi region on the Adriatic
coast of Italy are coming into their own as consumers discover what good values they are, especially the *rosso,* a deep, vivid red with meaty
flavors and just enough tannin to give it "grip."
Increasingly, large quantities of this wine mean
that some are less impressive; others can be excellent value, such as Rosso della Quercia, and
Riservas. Many also come in 1.5-liter magnums,
a good all-purpose red for parties.

Age: 1–3 years, the best last 4–6
Price: $5–8
Recommended Producers: Casal Thaulero ✪,
  Cornaccia, Dario d'Angelo, Duchi, Guelphi,

Illuminati, Monti, Bruno Nicodemi, Rosso della
Quercia, Sant'Angelo Rubino, Tuscolo, Valenti,
Valverde, Zaccagnini
Foods: Lamb stew, roast chicken, lasagne and other
meat pastas, pizza

Nebbiolo d'Alba

A sound red from the Nebbiolo grape, occasionally approaching the character of Barolo but
softer and lighter in body. Better wines labeled
Nebbiolo della Langhe are similar. CAUTION:
Both can be thin and hard in lesser vintages;
overpriced from some estates, rarely worth
more than $10 (exception: Luigi Einaudi, $18),
but those that cost more are sometimes found at
discount (♦).

Age: 2–4 years, may last 6–8
Price: $9–12
Recommended Producers: Elio Altare ♦, Cortese, S.
   Farina, Massolino, Oddero, Pio Cesare, Gigi
   Rosso
Foods: Roast chicken, veal stew, *ossobuco*

Refosco

Robust red made from the grape of that name
and a favorite hearty quaff in Friuli. Now more
widely seen here but curiously expensive. Occasionally can be overly tannic; Riservas are better
balanced but cost well over $12.

Age: 2–3, can go 5 or 6
Price: $7–9.50

Recommended Producers: Durandi, Franco Furlan, Pittaro

Foods: Hearty meat stews, game, savory cheeses

Rosso Cónero
Rosso Piceno

Two solid, meaty reds from the Marches region of central Italy made from Montepulciano and Sangiovese grapes. These *rossos* can be excellent value. Somewhat tannic when young but flavorful and well balanced, they often achieve some elegance with a few years in bottle.

Age: 3 years, will age 6–8

Price: $7–9

Recommended Producers: Bocca di Gabbia, Castelfiora, Cupramontana, Fazi-Battaglia, Garofoli, Marchetti, Moroder, Torelli, Umani Ronchi, Villa Pigna, Villamagna ✳

Foods: Lamb, beef, game birds, duck

Rosso di Montalcino

Firm, vigorous red wine from the Montalcino hills, traditionally made from young vines of Brunello di Montalcino, Tuscany's concentrated, noble (and expensive) red. Now may include lots of Brunello not good enough for the main label, as well as wines from vines under ten years old. The increasing popularity of the *rosso* has boosted prices beyond our limit for some of these wines, but it is often an excellent value from the estates cited.

Age: 2–5 years, can go 8–10

Price: $9–12 +

Recommended Producers: Altesino ♦, Argiano, Avignonesi ♦, Banfi Centine, Barbi, Bracesca, Boscarelli, Caparzo, Carpineto, Casanova di Neri, Col d'Orcia ☺, Dei, I Due Cipressi, La Gerla, La Lecciaia, Lisini ♦, Mastroianni, Nardi, La Poderina, Sesta, Terre di Priori, Val di Suga, Valdicava

Foods: Roast or grilled meats, stews, game, savory cheeses like aged Asiago, Parmigiano, Scamorze

Rosso del Salento

Strong, sturdy, tannic reds with a faintly bitter edge, from the Salento Peninsula in southern Italy. Often very ripe and high in alcohol (14 percent or better), particularly the best known, Notoparano, which needs six or seven years to become drinkable. Salice Salentino, which has its own DOC, is similar and made from the same grape (Negroamaro), but is a bit leaner and not as brawny. A better buy, in my view.

Age: 6–8 years, can age to 10 or 12

Price: $8–10

Recommended Producers: F. Candido, Colombo, Leone de Castris, Notoparano (Cosimo Taurino), Santachiara (Medico)

Foods: Meat stews, game, particularly venison, pecorino cheese

Rubesco

Solid, meaty red from the Lungarotti estate in Umbria. Made primarily from Sangiovese and drinkable within two to four years of the vintage; Riserva has more depth but costs more and ages eight to ten years.

Age: 2–4 years
Price: $10
Producer: Lungarotti
Foods: Roast meats, game birds, lasagne

Santa Maddalena

Fairly substantial red from the Tyrol region of Trentino in northern Italy; rich color, meaty flavors with a slight hint of bitterness; solid, occasionally complex; good value.

Age: 3 years, will age to 5 or 6
Price: $8–11
Recommended Producers: Josef Brigl, Kettmeir, Lageder, San Michele-Appiano
Foods: Meats, game, blood sausage, hearty pastas

Spanna

Earthy, full-bodied red from the Nebbiolo grape (called Spanna on the lower slopes at Gattinara; concentrated, even coarse, but ages for years (undrinkably tannic when under 7 or 8 years). Generous, expansive fruit, muscular in structure; well-stored old ones can be impressive, but are less a bargain than formerly; some are a better value than Gattinara.

Age: 4–5 years, will go to 10 or 15
Price: $8–12

Recommended Producers: Antoniolo, Brugo,
   Dessilani, Ferrando, Nervi, Travaglini, Vallana
Foods: Meat stews, especially venison, Gorgonzola

Valpolicella

Only the *classico superiore* is worth recommend-
ing, as ordinary Valpolicella is a modest and
often uninteresting light red. Wines from the better producers, however, are nicely balanced, medium-bodied, smooth, fruity reds that can be
genial with lighter foods. Beware very cheap
ones, which are often thin and lack character.
Amarone is this wine's bigger, tougher older
brother, made from grapes that are dried to concentrate flavor.

Age: 2 years, can go 3 or 4
Price: $8–11
Recommended Producers: Allegrini, Beatti, Bertani,
   Bolla, Boscaini, Guerrieri-Rizzardi, Le Salette,
   Masi, Mazzi, Santa Sofia, Speri, Tommasi
Foods: Calves' liver, pizza, ragout

Valtellina Superiore

The steep hills of the Valtellina district in Lombardy produce several sturdy reds from Nebbiolo that are similar in structure and flavor;
Grumello, Inferno, Sassella, Valgella, which are
frequently excellent value. Wines made from ex-
traripe grapes and aged longer go under the
name Sfurzat, which is very full-bodied and can
be somewhat raisiny. Valtellina Rosso, simple
but meaty and well balanced, is often a superb
value for events like barbecues, or large groups.

Age: 2–3 years, can go 4–6 or longer
Price: $6–12
Recommended Producers: Nino Negri, Nera,
   Rainoldi, Tona
Foods: Pizza, sausage and peppers, braised beef,
   ossobuco

ITALIAN ROSÉS

Italian *rosato,* as the rosés are called, can be charming. The best ones are dry, crisp, and refreshing; some even have character, such as Rosa del Golfo from Apulia. It's well to realize, however, that some Italian producers now sweeten their *rosatos* to please Americans who like sweet pink wines. Listed below are what I consider the best values in *dry rosatos.* They can accompany a variety of lighter foods, including cold meats, prosciutto, and simple fish. Drink them as young and fresh as possible, in their first or second year. Prices range from $6.99 to $10.

Castel del Monte Rosato, Apulia
Chiaretto del Garda, Veneto
Coltibuono Rosato, Tuscany
Costadolio, Veneto ✪
Lagrein Rosato, dei Conti Martini, Trentino
Regaleali Rosato, Sicily
Rosa dei Masi, Veneto
Rosa del Golfo, Apulia
Ruffino Clivo, Tuscany
Silvarosa, Giacosa Donato, Piedmont
Taurino Rosato di Salice Salentino

SUPERBUYS / ITALY

Whites

Anselmi Soave Classico, Veneto, $8

Antinori Orvieto Campogrande, Umbria, $9

Breganze di Breganze, Veneto, $12

Coltibuono Bianco, Tuscany, $8

Plozner Chardonnay, Friuli, $8.99

Ruffino Libaio, Tuscany, $7.99

J. Tiefenbrunner Chardonnay, Trentino, $7

Santi Lugana, Lombardy, $8.50

Vernaccia di San Gimignano, Tuscany (Angelo del
    Tufo, Teruzzi e Puthod), $8.99

Reds

Argiano Rosso di Montalcino, Tuscany, $10

Clerico Ginestrino, $9

Coltibuono Rosso, Tuscany, $7.50

Dessilani Barbera, $10

Felsina Chianti Classico, Tuscany, $10

Isole e Olena Chianti Classico, Tuscany, $11

Luiano Chianti Classico Riserva, $10

Monte Antico, Tuscany, $7.99–9

Rosé

Costadolio, Veneto, $8.99

4

Spain and Portugal

The best wines of Spain and Portugal are red, and both countries offer some amazing wine values. Portugal's robust, meaty, flavorful reds go for $5 and $6, several Superbuys (✪) among them. Spain's well-known Riojas and Penedés reds still offer a number of bargains among the growing number of more serious, and more expensive, wines.

White wines are made in copious quantities. Iberian wine producers have not taken white wines very seriously until recently, though Spain's Albariño is an outstanding exception. Portugal has its Vinho Verde, the young, tart "green wines" of the Minho region bordering the Douro. While they can be delightful and refreshing there, or in Lisbon, or at an oceanside restaurant watching the sunset, many are too light-bodied to travel well over greater distances. Other whites from Portugal and Spain exhibit a

new freshness of fruit and character that is most
appealing.

SPAIN

Some exciting new wines have already begun to
appear in Spain. American consumers are familiar with Spanish Rioja and with reds like Torres
Sangre de Toro and Coronas. In recent years
new vintners and winemakers have emerged
from other regions and appellations of this vast
country—the Ribera del Duero, Navarra, Rueda,
La Mancha, where innovative winemakers are
blending traditional grapes like Tempranillo and
Garnacha (Grenache) with Cabernet and Merlot. But consider: Spain is the third-largest producer of wine in the world, right on the heels of
France and Italy. It has more vineyard acreage
than either, but we hardly know Spanish wine.
Most of it is produced in bulk and consumed
within the country itself. La Mancha, for instance, produces over a third of Spanish wine,
almost all of it in the 450 cooperatives that dot
the region.

Get a taste of rich little reds like Lar de Barros
or Gran Colegiata Toro, which sell for $6 to $8 a
bottle, and you'll get a notion of what Spain can
do when a talented winemaker is at the helm.
Some of the new wines are expensive. Pesquera,
Viña Magaña, and most Ribera del Duero are
impressive and costly. In Rioja, too, the best
ones are costing more, but there are still numerous good buys for $10 to $12 and under.

CATALONIA

Catalonia produces some of Spain's best wines, especially the reds from the Penedés, including Cabernet Sauvignon from several producers and popular reds from the Torres firm such as Coronas and Sangre de Toro. West of Barcelona, near the town of San Sadurní de Noya, are the largest sparkling-wine producers in the world— Freixenet and Codorníu, as well as other names in Spanish *cavas* such as Juve y Camps, Segura Viudas ✪, Mont-Marçal, Lembey, and others.

The leading wines are listed separately.

Cabernet Sauvignon

Rich, earthy, but smooth and drinkable within three to five years for wines that are $9 to $11, though they can often hold longer; sometimes blended with the Spanish grape Tempranillo. *Recommended:* Mont-Marçal, Raimat, Joan Sarda, Jaume Serra.

Chardonnay

Chardonnay, now more widely grown in Catalonia, is used alone or in blends with local grapes Parellada and Macabeo. *Recommended:* Can Feixes Blanco Seleccio, Raimat, Joan Sarda, Torres Gran Viña Sol.

Coronas

A sound, medium-bodied red wine made from Tempranillo by the leading Penedés firm, Torres. Gran Coronas, blended with Cabernet, is meatier, with more concentrated fruit and flavor. (Gran Coronas Black Label, made from 100 percent Cabernet Sauvignon, is a wonderful wine but out of our league.)

Age: 2–4 years; 5–7 for Gran Coronas
Price: $6–10
Recommended Producers: Torres
Foods: Hamburgers, grilled chicken, beef

PRIORATO

This small mountain region near Tarragona produces some very pricey reds (such as Clos Erasmus), but a few supervalues have made their way here: Onix, a spicy blend of Carignan and Garnacha (Grenache), about $7, and the denser, berryish Scala dei Negri, about $7.50. *Foods:* Grilled meats, sausage, roast pork

Sangre de Toro

Another great value from Torres, Sangre de Toro is a robust, fruity red, immediately drinkable. Gran Sangre is even more so, full of berryish fruit and vigorous body that is excellent with hearty dishes like meat stews or barbecued meats.

Age: 2–3 years, up to 5 or more for the Gran Sangre
Price: $5–10
Foods: Hamburgers, grilled meats, chicken, sausage

TEMPRANILLO

Tempranillo is Spain's native grape for quality reds. The principal grape used in Rioja, it is also widely grown elsewhere and often blended with other varieties, such as Garnacha (Grenache) and Cabernet Sauvignon. Raimat produces it as a varietal as well as blended with Cabernet, as does Torres in Coronas and Gran Coronas, Mont-Marçal, and Can Feixes Negre Seleccio.

Viña Sol

A dry, fruity white from Torres, simple but fresh and well made. Not to be confused with Chardonnay-based Gran Viña Sol ✪, a terrific value and one of the best Spanish whites.

Age: 1–3 years
Price: $7–10
Sole Producer: Torres
Foods: Mild fish and seafood

GALICIA

This region of northern Spain is best known for the superb dry white Albariño (see). Several of the region's cooperatives make attractive light wines such as the lightly sparkling *(pétillant)* Pazo white and red, as well as Oro Ribeiro, Valdamor, and Viña Costeira. None are widely seen in the United States as yet.

Albariño

This scintillating white wine, perhaps the best in Spain, certainly the most interesting and unique. Made from the Albariño grape grown in Galicia, it is notable for crisp, bright fruit and a flowery scent hinting of apples, pears, and delicate blossoms. The best are expensive ($17–21), but a few—slightly less scintillating but appealing—can be found for about $12.

Age: 1–3 years
Price: $12
Recommended Producers: Cervara Hermanos, Martin Codax ✪, Fillaboa, Pazo de Señorans
Foods: Delightful aperitif or with trout

LAR DE BARROS

This chewy, drinkable red from Extremadura in western Spain is an excellent value from the province's only official appellation, Tierra de Barros. Rich, sturdy fruit makes it a Superbuy ✪.

Age: 4–6 years, will go 10
Price: $8.50
Producer: Bodegas Enviosa Lar de Barros ✪
Foods: Roast or grilled meats, meat stews, savory cheeses such as Manchego

---

LA MANCHA

Huge quantities of nondescript wines are produced in La Mancha, much of it in bulk that supplies everyday wines all over Spain. The plains of La Mancha have more than a million acres in vines, constituting Spain's largest appellation. Best known in the United States are jugs of Valdepeñas, light reds that are usually served chilled in Spain to make them more refreshing and quaffable. A few producers make sturdier reds of firmer structure aged in oak (Felix Solis) that may soon find their way here.

NAVARRA

Navarra, north of the Rioja and west of Catalonia, produces reds similar to Rioja from some of the same grapes, Garnacha (Grenache) and Tempranillo. Supple, generously fruity new reds have emerged here recently, offering good everyday drinking value. Be on the watch also for Navarra's dry, bracing rosés (labeled *rosado*), great favorites of Hemingway on his frequent trips to Pamplona.

Age: 2–4 years
Price: $5–7.50
Recommended Producers: Las Campañas Navarra Crianza, Chivite Reserva and Gran Fuedo, Bodegas Guelbenzu, Magaña-Barillas Eventum, Señorio de Sarria Reserva ✪, Torrecilla
Foods: Grilled meats, hamburgers, cheese

RIBERA DEL DUERO

This region, west of the Rioja and near Valladolid in Castilla-León, produces Spain's most intense and expensive red, Vega Secilia, which sells for $50 to $60 a bottle. Other producers have sprung up, a few producing hearty reds more in our price range, but often quite meaty and long-lived. Watch for them on sale or at discount stores.

Age: 4–10 years, or longer

Price: $8–10 + ✳

Recommended Producers: Hijos de Antonio
   Barcelo, Mesoneros de Castilla, Bodegas de
   Mollina, Penalba ✪, Señorio de Nava,
   Torremilanos, Bodegas Valduero, Viña Mayor

Foods: Steak, grilled meats, meat stews

RIOJA

Spain's best-known wine region, producing red
wines of the same name. There are dozens of
producers, about forty of which export to the
United States. Variations in quality abound.
Some of the top estates can command higher
prices, putting their Reservas and Gran Reservas
fairly well out of reach. Young Rioja (released
after two years, it is called Crianza) is medium-
bodied, fruity, and rather light. Reservas, aged
four to six years, are riper and bigger, as are
Gran Reservas (expensive), which are the best
lots of a superior vintage. Competition has
heated up in the last few years, and quality
seems to be improving among the leading producers, with good values at the simple level, even
better ones among Reservas, which are frequently found marked down.

Age: 3–5 years for Crianza, 5–10 for Reservas,
   Gran Reservas, and some beyond that

Price: $6–12 +

Recommended Producers: Berberana, Bilbainas,
   Bosconia, Campo Viejo, Conde de Valdemar ✪,
   CUNE, Grand Condal, Lopez de Heredia, Breton
   Loriñon ✪, Marqués de Arienzo, Marqués de
   Cáçeres, Marqués de Murrieta, Marqués de

Riscal, Martinez-Bujanda, Montecillo, Bodegas
Palacio Glorioso, Paternina, La Rioja Alta,
Valdemar, Viña Tondonia
Foods: Lamb, beef, savory cheeses like Manchego

Rioja White and Rosado

Improved vineyard and winemaking techniques
have mightily upgraded the quality of Rioja
whites and rosés. Virtually all the firms known
for quality produce good, fresh white wines
(Blanco) and attractive dry rosés *(Rosado)*. They
are best when young, one or two years at most.
Both wines are versatile with light foods and as
aperitifs.

RUEDA

Another region in Castilla-León, up and coming
for crisp, dry, flavorful white wines made from
the Verdejo grape. Much more stylish and appealing than Rioja Blanco—perhaps the reason
several Rioja producers are now making their
whites there.

Age: 1–3 years
Price: $7–10
Recommended Producers: Marqués de Griñon ♦,
   Marqués de Riscal, Martinsancho ✪, Martivilli,
   Vega de la Reina
Foods: Fish, seafood

TORO ✪

This new region in Castilla-León is creating a lot
of excitement with its bargain-priced hearty reds

like Gran Colegiata, an amazing buy at $5! Toro is hot, so prices will undoubtedly rise, but perhaps not too high too fast. Snap them up! And watch for new labels that may appear.

Age: 3–10 years
Price: $5–6
Recommended Producers: Fariña Gran Colegiata ✪,
   Luis Mateos Vega de Toro ✪
Foods: Hearty meat dishes

OTHER GOOD BUYS

Spain has many excellent values from various parts of this large country. The ones below are highly recommended and include a few Superbuys.

Carchelo Monastrell, Murcia ✪, $6, plump,
   juicy red from the Mourvèdre grape; lots of
   flavor.
Palacio de Leon Tinto, $5, firm, deep, and
   tannic, with good aging potential.
Montesierra Somontano, $7, Spain's answer to
   Beaujolais, light, fruity, and appealing; the
   white is fresh and lively.
Estola La Mancha Reserva, $6–8, berryish fruit,
   with toasty oak overtones; very drinkable.
René Barbier Family Reserve Red ✪, $6.50, top
   bargain for everyday red.
Taja Jumilla Tinto ✪, $5, robust, lively, and
   fruity.
Vega de la Reina Crianza, $7, stylish Rioja-like
   red from Valladolid.
Viñas del Vero Somontano, $8–9, lively whites
   and fruity reds from Pyrénées foothills.

PORTUGAL

As in Spain, it is the red wines of Portugal that generate the most interest—astonishment, actually. What a shock to find rich, meaty, powerfully structured reds with such incredibly cheap price tags! At full markup some rarely go beyond $7.99 a bottle; often they are priced well below that at $5 and $6. Certainly they are among the most undervalued of wines—or is it just that we have gotten used to *over*priced wines? While the latter is undeniably true, there are other factors at work. One has to do with image. Portuguese reds lack the slick image of wines from Italy, France, or California that may be comparable in style but can command higher prices. People see the low prices for wines like Dão, Serradayres, Periquita, and various Garrafeiras, and wonder how they can be any good.

Those who have discovered the good ones, however, feel they have been let in on a great secret and are delighted by the bold, robust flavors. That brings up another factor. Most Portuguese reds are rustic and full-bodied, dark, and often rather tannic, and thus not to everyone's taste. If you like that style, however, you will find some extraordinary buys. Portuguese reds can be very long-lived. You will see many wines that are ten to fifteen years old, but most are drinkable when they arrive here, and often quite glorious. Some, however, have spent too long in wood, and you may find they have lost fruit or dried up. The recent trend is to emphasize fruit rather than wood, producing wines that are ready to drink within a few years but can age a decade or more. Keep an eye on Portugal. It is a wine industry that is starting to churn with new

energy, and some Portuguese vintners are beginning to produce reds with more finesse. Prices
for some of them are already on the rise.

In Portugal wines go by regional appellation,
such as Dão or Bairrada, but many are better
known by producer or by proprietary names.
This is especially true for reds from the regions
of Ribatejo and Alentejo, for example. The wines
recommended are listed alphabetically by region, type, producer, or brand name, depending
upon which identity is strongest and most easily
recognized.

ALENTEJO

This large region southeast of Lisbon near the
Spanish border is best known for medium- to
full-bodied red wines, and whites of lesser interest. Large cooperatives such as Borba, Re-
guengos de Monsaraz, and Redondo make solid,
meaty reds that are very good value, but serious
estates have begun to appear in recent years.
The future promises some exciting wines.

Age: 5–8 years
Price: $5–8
Recommended Producers: Borba, Borba Reserva ✪,
    Herdade de Esporão Tinto, Herdade de Santa
    Marta Tinto, Redondo Real Lavrador, Reguengos
    de Monsaraz, Reguengos Reserva ✪, J. P. Vinhos
    Anfora
Foods: Hearty meat dishes, game, stews, savory
    cheeses

Anfora ✪

Rich, full-bodied red from the Palmela district of
Alentejo. Ripe flavors, soft tannins, a Superbuy
from J. P. Vinhos.

Age: 3–5 years, will go to 8 or 10
Price: $7
Producer: J. P. Vinhos
Foods: Grilled meats, stews, savory cheeses

BAIRRADA

A region along Portugal's central coast north of
Lisbon noted for well-balanced red wines, especially Reservas. These reds are some of Portugal's most elegant, sometimes compared to
Bordeaux in terms of structure and style. There
are excellent values here, but prices for some
wines are inching beyond $10.

Age: 5–10 years, longer for Reservas
Price: $8–10 +
Recommended Producers: Caves Aliança Garrafeira
   and Galeria (white), Dom Teodosio Reserva ✪,
   Frei João Reserva ✪, Luis Pato (also João Pato),
   Quinta de Pedralvites, Caves São João ✪, Porta
   Ferrea, Caves Primavera, Sogrape Terra Franca
   ✪ (also Terra Franca Garrafeira), Souselas
   Reserva, Caves Velhas
Foods: Grilled or roast lamb or beef, prime rib

BUCELAS

A small region near Lisbon that produces dry white wines of medium body. Few reach the United States, though recent plantings in the region may change that. Look for the Arinto label.

Casal de Azenha ✪

B. Paulo da Silva's brand name for a ripe, meaty red from vineyards near the region of Colares (see below). Deep and long-lived (ten to fifteen years).

Age: 10–15 years
Price: $7–10
Sole Producer: B. Paulo da Silva
Foods: Game, meat stews

Catarina ✪

A very attractive dry white wine from J. P. Vinhos; fruity, crisp, and flavorful, with a hint of Chardonnay in the blend.

Age: 1–2 years
Price: $6
Producer: J. P. Vinhos
Foods: Fish, seafood

COLARES

This small region on the Atlantic coast above Lisbon was once noted for dark, rich reds that needed many years of aging. Recent wines are lighter, fruitier, and more supple; agreeably good, but rarely more—exception: Casal de Azenha, a Superbuy from vineyards just inland from Colares.

Age: 5–10 years
Price: $5–8
Recommended Producers: B. Paulo da Silva,
    Tavares y Rodrigues
Foods: Beef, lamb, meat stews

Cova da Ursa ☉

A wood-aged Chardonnay from the firm of J. P. Vinhos; one of Portugal's best dry whites, evidence of the country's potential for superior white wine.

Age: 2–4 years
Price: $9–12
Producer: J. P. Vinhos
Foods: Fish, shellfish, veal or chicken in cream
    sauce

DÃO

One of Portugal's oldest and best-known regions for sturdy, full-bodied red wines, and to a lesser extent, dry whites. In northern Portugal, just south of the Douro region, it is a region somewhat in transition. Traditionally the hearty red Dão were given lengthy aging in cask, resulting in heavy, tannic wines that tasted more of wood than of fruit. Quality still varies among the numerous large producers who buy grapes and bottle the wines under brand names. There are, however, some excellent Reservas and Garrafeiras. For a long time the only estate was Conde de Santar (a Superbuy), but now other producers have purchased vineyards that will appear under estate names. Be wary of wines over eight to ten years old. Dão can certainly age at least that, but some wines may be dried out.

Age: 5-8 years, longer for Reservas, Garrafeiras
Price: $7-12
Recommended Producers: Caves Aliança, Borges & Irmão Meia Encosta, Conde de Santar ✪, Dom Teodosio Cardeal Reserva, Fonseca Terras Altas ✪, Grão Vasco Reserva, Porta Dos Cavaleiros Reserva, Sogrape Duque de Viseu, Caves Velhas Garrafeira ✪
Foods: Feijoada (Brazilian meat stew) and other robust meat dishes, savory cheeses

---

DOURO

The steep slopes of the Douro Valley in northern Portugal are most famous for Port, the fabulous fortified red. But a few producers also make red table wine that is big, deep, and dark, as one might expect from this rugged region. Very concentrated Douro reds, such as Barca Velha, are now quite expensive, but a few can be found within our price range.

Age: Drinkable at 5-8 years but often need much longer
Price: $9-10 +
Recommended Producers: Caves Accacio Reserva,

Casal de Valle Pradinhas, Ferreirinha Esteva ✪
and Vinha Grande, Quinta de la Rosa, Quinta do
Cotto

Garrafeira, Reserva, Particular

Many producers make a Garrafeira, or proprietor's reserve, which is their best. The wine may be made from the best lots of a regional wine such as Bairrada or Dão, or it may be a nonspecific blend of exceptional wines. Some are labeled Garrafeira Particular, others Reserva Particular (*Particular* is not an official term). Wines from top producers such as those listed below are deep, rich, well balanced, and long-lived. They are some of the best Portugal has to offer, yet rarely exceed $12 a bottle.

Age: 7–10 years, can go 12
Price: $7.50–12
Recommended Producers: Caves Aliança, Antonio
    Bernardino, Carvalho Ribeiro & Ferreira ✪,
    Casaleiro, Caves Dom Teodosio, B. Paulo da Silva,
    Caves São João ✪, Caves Velhas ✪
Foods: Roast meats, venison, boar, pheasant, wild
    duck

João Pires ✪

Brand name for Caves João Pires White Muscat, a dry, delightfully fruity white that is Portugal's top buy in white wine. Fresh, crisp, and fragrant, with the enticing floral/spice aromas and flavors of Muscat at its best. What sets this wine apart from all other Portuguese whites is that it is utterly clean and beautifully balanced. Drink it

young, within a year of the vintage if possible,
when the fruit is freshest.

Age: 6–18 months
Price: $6.50–9
Producer: João Pires
Foods: Great by itself

Periquita ✪

An excellent meaty red produced by José Maria
da Fonseca from the Periquita grape. Fonseca
made the Periquita famous with this wine, one
of Portugal's best-known reds and a Superbuy at
$7. Now, others have become available.

Age: 5–10 years or longer
Price: $7–10
Producer: José Maria da Fonseca, Quinta de
    Parrotes, Quinta de São João Batista, Quinta do
    Bairro Salcão
Foods: Lamb, beef, meat stews

Quinta da Camarate Clarete

A light, fruity red from the J. M. Fonseca firm at
Azeitão, made in part with Cabernet Sauvignon.
Good value.

Age: 2–4 years
Price: $5
Producer: J. M. Fonseca Sucrs.
Foods: Roast chicken, sausages

Quinta da Folgorosa

A very fine estate red from the north-central hills
of the Torres Vedras region. Folgorosa, owned

by the excellent firm of Carvalho, Ribeiro & Ferreira, produces a rich ruby red, full of spicy, cherrylike fruit braced with firm tannins that make it seem more robust than it is.

Age: 4–8 years
Price: $7
Producer: Quinta da Folgorosa
Foods: Roast beef, game birds, goat cheese

Quinta de Abrigada

A robust red from Portugal's eastern frontier region of Extremadura. Very good, especially the Garrafeira.

Age: 5–8 years, longer for the Garrafeira
Price: $7–10
Producer: Quinta de Abrigada
Foods: Grilled meats, game

Quinta de Pancas

A robust red with plenty of flavor from the Alenquer region north of Lisbon. The estate Cabernet Sauvignon is also quite good. Both about $7.

RIBATEJO

A region northeast of Lisbon in the province of Extremadura bordering Spain. Several superb values in red wines are made here, better known by brand names than by the regional name, such as Romeira and Serradayres. Sturdy, rich, often rather Rhône-like in their ripe, oaky flavors and powerful structure.

Age: 4–7 years, Garrafeiras will go 10 or more
Price: $5–8
Recommended Producers: **Carvalho, Ribeiro & Ferreira Serradayres Tinto ✪ (the white is also agreeable), C., R. & F. Garrafeira, Dom Teodosio Casaleiro Velho, Falcoaria (red and white ✪), Quinta da Lagoalva, Quinta do Alorna, Romeira and Romeira Garrafeira ✪, Caves Velhas**
Foods: **Roast meats, game, meat stews**

Serradayres ✪

One of the top values in Portuguese reds, this full-bodied, richly textured wine is from a vineyard overlooking the Tagus River in the Ribatejo (see) region bordering Spain. Produced by Carvalho, Ribeiro & Ferreira, Serradayres is the name of the vineyard and means "mountain of air." Well balanced, flavorful and highly drinkable, it goes for the rather amazing price of $5 a bottle! The beefier Tras-Os-Montes is about $8.

Vinho Verde

These very light-bodied, crisp whites (*vinho verde* literally means "green wines") from the northern region of the Minho River can be delightful in Portugal, tart and briskly dry, fresh and bracing. Unfortunately, few taste as good when they arrive here in the United States. They are frequently either oversulphured or sweetened to make them seem less austere. Both practices defeat the purpose; prices have gone up as well, unjustifiably in my view, so I recommend very few of these wines.

Age: 12–18 months
Price: $5–8.50
Recommended Producers: Aveleda Grinalda, Casal Garcia, Casaleiro, Gazela, Paco de Teixeiro

FORTIFIED WINES

In Sherry, Port, and Madeira, Spain and Portugal produce the world's greatest fortified wines, altogether unique in character. They are imitated in wine regions the world over, but most of the imitators fall well short of the prototypes. There are not many that can be recommended here because prices have risen in recent years. But there are certain ones that fall within our $12 limit, and I strongly urge you to try them. You'll probably want to keep a bottle or two on hand.

Many Sherries cost under $12 a bottle, though the best have risen beyond that; here, I only recommend those that I consider truly superior buys.

As for Port, few indeed can be found for $12— that I would recommend, at any rate. Most of the Port shippers produce inexpensive wood-aged Ports labeled Ruby, Tawny, or White Port. But it's better to spend a dollar or two more and get a Reserve-style wood Port, as recommended below (♦). Real Tawny Ports are costly, usually considerably more than $12—don't be fooled by Tawnies that are actually blends of Ruby and White Port.

Madeira, long undervalued, is also rising in

price as consumers discover how delectable it can be. The rich, golden sweet Malmseys have jumped to $20 and $30 a bottle or more, especially those ten years or older. The lighter Rainwaters, Verdelhos, and Sercials often go for $11 to $12 but occasionally can be found for less. Catalonia's Malvasía de Sitges, about $11, is a delicious Madeira-like dessert wine.

Sherry

Emilio Lustau Fino (dry)
Emilio Lustau Palo Cortado (off-dry)
Gonzales Byass Tio Pepe Fino (dry
Hidalgo Amontillado (dry)
Hidalgo Cream (sweet)
Hidalgo Manzanilla (dry)
Hidalgo Oloroso (dry)
Pedro Domecq Celebration Cream (sweet)
Pedro Domecq La Ina Fino (dry)
Sandeman Armada Cream
Sandeman Character Oloroso (off-dry, rich)
Vinicola Hidalgo La Gitana Manzanilla (dry)

Port (wood-aged)

Cockburn Special Reserve *
Fonseca Bin 27 *
Sandeman Founder's Reserve *
Warre's Warrior *

Madeira (Rainwater, Verdelho, Sercial, Bual, Malmsey)

Blandy (Duke series)
Cossart Gordon
Leacock
Malvasía de Sitges
J. Robert

SUPERBUYS / SPAIN AND PORTUGAL

Spanish White
Torres Gran Viña Sol, $9
Marqués de Riscal Rueda, $7.50
Martin Codex Albariño, $12
Martinsancho Rueda, $7.99

Spanish Red
Bodegas Guelbenzu
Carchelo Monastrell-Mourvèdre, $7
Lar de Barros, $8.50
Rioja (Berberana, Loriñon, Conde de Valdemar),
   $6-8
René Barbier Family Reserve Red Table Wine,
   $6.50
Toro Fariña Gran Colegiata, $5
Taja Jumilla Tinto, $5
Montesierra Somontano, $5.50
Emilio Lustau Sherry (Fino, Palo Cortado),
   $11-12
Hidalgo Manzanilla, Oloroso, $8-10

Portugal White
Cova da Ursa Chardonnay, $7.99
João Pires Catarina, $6
João Pires White Muscat, $6
Falcoaria Almeirim, $9

Portugal Red
Borba Reserva, $7
João Pires Anfora, $6.99
Bairrada (Caves São João, Frei João Reserva,
   Terra Franca, Dom Teodosio Reserva), $7-11
Casal de Azenha, $8
Conde de Santar Dão, $9
Ferreirinha Esteva Douro, $9-11
Fonseca Terras Altas, $8

Garrafeira (Carvalho, Ribeiro & Ferreira, Caves
   São João, Caves Velhas), $7.50–12
Fonseca Perequita, $6–7
Quinta de Pancas, $8–10
Romeira Garrafeira, $7.49
Serradayres Tinto, $6–7
Cave Velhas Dão Garrafeira, $7.99

5

Eastern Europe and the Mediterranean

Many wine drinkers have wondered if *perestroika* will result in a more copious flow of wine from Eastern Europe. Undoubtedly it will, though it may take a year or so more for new developments to make an appearance here. For years, varietals from Romania and Bulgaria have offered good value, especially for Cabernet Sauvignon, Merlot, and Chardonnay of Bulgaria. These wines sell for $4 to $5 a bottle—rock-bottom prices, but it wouldn't matter a hoot if the wines were less than decent. The Romanian Premiat wines are at least that; the Bulgarian varietals are often considerably better. A few from other Eastern bloc countries, such as Cabernet Franc from Hungary, Cabernet and Merlot from the former Yugoslavia, are also surprisingly good, and have the potential to be even better.

Here in the West we have a lot to learn about Eastern European wines. These countries have, in fact, a tradition of winegrowing that goes back several centuries. Though most of the wine is produced at large, state-owned wineries, favorable microclimates and highly regarded vineyards do exist. Such vintners as Antinori of Tuscany, Jean-Michel Cazes of Bordeaux, and others have begun ventures in Hungary, Bulgaria, and Moldova. New plantings of popular varietals (Chardonnay, Merlot, Pinot Noir, the Cabernets) as well as classic techniques of vinification and aging in small oak barrels are already under way. In the future we can expect to see more oak-aged wines and Reserve wines that are higher in quality.

EASTERN EUROPE

Austria

Austria is making a slow comeback in the United States after several years of retrenching. Not many Austrian wines are available here now, but the quality is good. Look for fresh, light German-style whites with names like Grüner Veltliner, Gumpoldskirchener, and Rieslings from leading wine towns like Krems, Oggauer, and Rust. Austria produces lovely late-harvest, Botrytised Rieslings; many labeled Auslese are underpriced and excellent value. Austria is also experimenting with some success in red wines made from Cabernet Sauvignon, Merlot, Pinot Blanc, and Pinot Noir.

Fritz Salomon, Siegendorf, Höpler and Terry Theise Selections are among the top labels to look for in the United States.

Bulgaria

Trakia's meaty Cabernet Sauvignon (✪) and dry, full-bodied Chardonnay (✪) are two Superbuys, as lots of American wine lovers have already discovered. New efforts with Reserve-style wines and barrel-fermented, oak-aged whites are under way in Bulgaria, which promise to bring us even more interesting and complex wines. Be on the lookout for new labels. Currently Chardonnay and Cabernet Sauvignon labeled Balkan Crest represent decent values at around $6. Trakia Riesling and Merlot Blush are simple and adequate. Best buys ($4.29–5) are

    Trakia Cabernet Sauvignon ✪: meaty, flavorful, well balanced

    Trakia Chardonnay ✪: dry, lively, fruity, good balance and Chardonnay character

Hungary

Don't judge Hungarian wines by the popular red labeled Egri Bikavér (Bull's Blood), now a pallid version of the staunch red it used to be. It ranges from average to good but is not consistent. Newer, more vigorous and flavorful reds are being made from Cabernet Franc, Merlot, and Cabernet Sauvignon. These wines are not widely available yet, but they are good value. Dry Tokay Számarodni, such as that of Dísnoko, a new label, can be pleasantly fruity and crisp. The most famous Tokay is sweet and the best is expensive. Avoid the cheap ones, which are quite mediocre.

Recommended: Cabernet Franc, Cabernet
   Sauvignon, Merlot Old Vines ✪ in reds; Furmint,
   Gewurztraminer, and Tokay Számorodni in
   whites
Price: $7–10

Romania

Romania makes far more wine than you would
guess based on what is available here. Varietals
shipped under the Premiat brand include attractive but mild Cabernet Sauvignon and Merlot,
and fair-to-average Sauvignon Blanc and Chardonnay. The Tarnave Riesling, however, is mediocre, and the Pinot Noir quite light. It remains to
be seen if Romania can come up with wines as
impressive as those of Bulgaria.

Recommended: Premiat Cabernet Sauvignon,
   Merlot
Price: $4–6

Yugoslavia

Regions of the former Yugoslavia have loads of
potential for producing exceptional wine. Traditional reds from native grapes like Babíc, Plavac,
and Prokupac are robust and meaty, unusual,
and often distinctive. Considerable promise,
however, lies with such varieties as Cabernet,
Merlot, Sauvignon Blanc, Pinot Blanc and Chardonnay. Good, lively reds made from Merlot and
Cabernet Sauvignon are being produced in Istria
and Slovenia. The Dalmatian coast (Croatia) still
produces meaty reds such as Dingac, Faros, and
Plavac. We see little in the United States as yet,
but are sure to in the future.

Recommended: Avia, Nadia
Price: $3–5

THE MEDITTERANEAN

Greece (including Cyprus), Israel, Algeria, even
Lebanon, export wine to the United States. Mo-
rocco also produces wine, but it is not available
here, though there are agreeable light reds and
rather better dry rosés that are quite pleasant to
drink there.

Greece, where according to legend the gods
first gave wine to man, has been making it so
long that the Greeks seem rather laid-back about
the whole thing. Most Greek wine is at least pal-
atable (except perhaps for the acquired taste of
Retsina, the resinated Greek specialty), but
lately a few enterprising producers have begun
to revive ancient distinctive grape varieties (such
as Xinomavro Naoussis) and, in some cases, use
popular grapes like Cabernet, Merlot, and Syrah
to blend with them. The results are stylish new
wines that offer more flavor and character than
simple reds and whites like Demestica, the most
widely distributed Greek wines.

GREECE

Things are looking up for Greek wine. Producers
of stylish reds and whites like Boutari are likely
to prompt a general upgrading of quality as these
wines gain wider acceptance. The wines of
Greece and the island of Cyprus are known
mostly by producer, labeled with descriptive
(Dry Red), regional (Naoussa), or proprietary

names (Lac des Roches). There are also a few
generics, such as Retsina, Roditys, Mavro-
daphne, or Commanderia. Listings are by the
name most appropriate.

Boutari

Producer of several wines of top quality, both
white and red, made in styles for immediate
drinking. Some of the reds, such as Boutari
Grande Reserve or Naoussa, are capable of aging
a few years in bottle. Boutari has been dedicated
to reviving some of the ancient Greek grape varieties, such as the sturdy red Xinomavro from
Naoussa or the Negoska, produced in regions of
Macedonia. The firm also produces attractive
dry white wines, the best among them being Lac
des Roches.

Age: **Immediately drinkable**
Price: **$5–7.50**
Recommended Wines: **Red: Cava, Goumenissa,
    Grande Reserve, Naoussa, Paros, Patmos. White:
    Lac des Roches, Kretikos, Santorini**
Foods: **Lamb, grilled meats with the reds; with the
    white, fish, seafood, chicken, roasted or grilled
    vegetables**

Carras

Porto Carras is another producer of interesting
new wines that bear watching, particularly the
vigorous, Bordeaux-like Chateau Carras red and
the Carras Reserve dry white. Chateau Carras,
made from Cabernet Sauvignon, is quite tannic
in some vintages, and age-worthy. This large estate also produces several soft, drinkable, and

attractive wines under the Côtes de Meliton label.

Age: Immediately drinkable, though Chateau Carras
   will age a decade
Price: $4–6
Recommended Wines: Carras Reserve Dry White,
   Carras Rosé Special, Chateau Carras, Domaine
   Carras Vin Rouge
Foods: Reds: Grilled meats, hamburgers, pizza;
   White, rosé: shellfish, cold chicken, picnic foods

Commanderia

The sweet amber dessert wine of Cyprus dates
back several hundred years to the days of Richard the Lion-hearted, who once visited the island. All the top firms make the wine, which gets
its distinctive character from grapes laid out on
mats to dry and concentrate in the sun. Though
not fortified, it is fairly alcoholic, up to 15 percent. Smooth and not overly sweet, the best ones
make delicious dessert wines.

Age: Immediately drinkable but can keep several
   months
Price: $10 +
Recommended Producers: Etko, Keo, Loel, Sodap
Foods: Desserts, dried fruit, light cake or cookies;
   alone

Keo

One of the leading producers on Cyprus. Keo's
best labels are the dry, crisp white Aphrodite
and the firm, flavorful red Domaine d'Ahera.

Mavrodaphne

The sweet red wine made from the Mavro-
daphne grape. Rich and full-bodied, it can be
delightful when well made, but very cheap ones
can be disappointing.

Age: **Immediately drinkable**
Price: **$5-7**
Recommended Producers: **Achaia Clauss, Boutari,
    Bouzouki**
Foods: **Savory cheese or by itself after dinner**

Nemea

An appellation on the Corinthian Plain in the
Peloponnese producing sturdy, firm-structured
reds, often with a lion depicted on the label. Her-
cules, remember, slew the lion of Nemea.

Retsina

The Greek specialty, resin-flavored and pretty
much an acquired taste. Boutari makes the best
one, which is dry, well balanced, and fruity without an excess of the resin taste.

Age: **1-2 years**
Price: **$3-3.25**
Recommended Producers: **Boutari ✳, Cambas**

Robola of Cephalonia

This fragrant, appealing dry white, made from
the Robola grape, comes from the island of Ceph-
alonia in the Adriatic.

Rosé

Greece makes brisk, dry rosé; the best currently is Roditys, which has firm, rather austere fruit with a slight bite. It is quite refreshing, however, and is versatile with a variety of Greek foods. Amazingly cheap.

Age: **1–2 years, the younger the better**
Price: **$2–4**
Recommended Producers: **Boutari, Cambas Roditys, Carras Rosé Special, Rotonda Rosé**
Foods: **Greek appetizers, stewed lamb, feta cheese**

Naoussa and Goumenissa

These two regions in Macedonia in northern Greece produce some of the country's best reds, mostly from Xinomavro, the grape that yields medium-bodied reds as well as richer dark ones that age quite well. Labels to look for: Boutari Hatzi-Michalis, and Tsantali.

Samos

A sweet white Muscat made on the island of Samos, and quite a delicious way to end a Greek meal or savor a summer afternoon. It is usually served barely cool, yet isn't cloying.

Age: **Immediately drinkable**
Price: **$5–7**
Producer: **Cooperatives Vinicoles de Samos**
Foods: **Light cake or cookies; preferably by itself or with fresh fruit**

ISRAEL

Tremendous development has taken place in Israel in the last decade or so. The better wines come largely from Galilee and the cool slopes of the Golan Heights. Large quantities of wine are still produced in the Carmel Valley, where the Rothschild family planted vineyards in the 1880s. Israel's best wines are crisp, dry whites—such as Sauvignon Blanc, Chenin Blanc, and Chardonnay —and Cabernet Sauvignon that is medium-bodied and easy to drink, as well as deeper wines aged in oak.

Recommended Producers: **Baron, Carmel Vineyard Varietals, Gamla, Golan, and Yarden**

6

United States

California produces 90 percent of the wines made in America. Since California wines are also the most widely distributed of American wines, they make up the bulk of the listings in this chapter. In recent years, however, five other states— New York, Oregon, Texas, Virginia, and Washington—have made impressive strides. Chardonnay, Merlot, Pinot Noir, Riesling, and other varietals from these states often exhibit a quality and individual style that approaches world-class. Wines with reasonable national distribution are included where appropriate, without reference to their origin. Following these listings is a section on good values from these and other states.

Except for the growing category of premium blends with proprietary names (expensive wines like Opus One, Rubicon, Carmenet, Le Cigare de Volant), America's best wines are labeled with varietal names, as alphabetized below—Cab-

ernet Sauvignon, Chardonnay, Chenin Blanc,
etc. There are no jugs, as such, included here,
though some of the wines recommended come in
1.5-liter magnums. This is not a reflection of
some kind of snobbism. Jug wines, especially generics labeled Burgundy, Chablis, Vin Rosé, and
the like, once offered good value in American
wines. Fairly decent grapes sometimes went into
them. Today, however, jugs have declined in
both quality and popularity for various reasons.
One is that people want more flavor and character in the wine they drink, even on an everyday
basis. The generic jugs are bland, lacking in character, and often lacking in freshness and liveliness. Further, they are rarely vintage-dated, so
that you have no idea how old they actually are.
Many are pasteurized to keep them stable and
give them long shelf life. This treatment robs
them of any character or style they might possess
and makes them quite dull. Though they are
cheap, there is rarely anything beyond that to
recommend them. Some producers are aware of
this perception of their product; perhaps we
shall see some renewed efforts at improvement,
but I am not hopeful.

In their place we have a few premium generic
blends made from the better grape varieties like
Cabernet, Chardonnay, Gewurztraminer, Sauvignon Blanc, and others, such as Clos du Val
Le Clos, Preston Estate Red, and The Monterey
Vineyard Classics. The best of these wines are
included in Proprietary Reds and Proprietary
Whites. The big change in California wine over
the last two decades has been the shift to varietal
wines. Today there are a multitude of moderate-
priced varietals, some as bland and charac-
terless as any of the jugs, to be sure, but others
that offer good to outstanding value at prices

ranging from $4 to $10. This category has ballooned phenomenally in recent years.

Certain varietal wines have always been $10 and under. Wines like Sauvignon Blanc, Pinot Blanc, Zinfandel, Petite Sirah, Chenin Blanc, Johannisberg or White Riesling have usually cost less than Cabernet Sauvignon, Chardonnay, Merlot, and Pinot Noir, often well under $10. In the early 1980s, due to a surplus of good-quality Cabernet and Chardonnay, a new category of moderate-priced Cabernets and Chardonnays emerged. Some were second labels of well-known premium wineries, such as the Liberty School label of Caymus.

Priced at $5 to $7, these wines were dubbed the "fighting varietals"—a sobriquet that took note of their fiercely competitive pricing. Restaurants began pouring them by the glass, especially Chardonnay. People soon learned that Chardonnay offered more flavor than the average "house" white. Gradually consumers looking to move beyond the jugs discovered these less expensive varietals, and they have become a solid category that now includes Merlot, Pinot Noir, and Sauvignon Blanc, as well as premium generic blends.

Quality varies within this large group of wines. Not all of them are good, by any means, but recommended here are those I have found to be consistently so—so far. I am, however, disappointed in two developments related to the fighting varietals. First, some have not maintained their quality as production has increased.

Second, several of the best-sellers have started making "Reserve" wines that sell for $10 or more. Some of these wines are rip-offs—harsher, more tannic Cabernets, oakier, more alcoholic Chardonnays, and nowhere near as drinkable as the regular wines. Worse, some of the regular wines from these producers are now being compromised because the so-called Reserves are skimming off the best grapes. This is commercialism at its worst. Prices overall have risen a bit. The quality of some labels, however, has gone up, making them better buys today. The $7 to $12 niche is really the engine that drives the American wine market.

Cabernet Sauvignon

Cabernet is California's best red grape, produced in a broad range of styles, including deeply colored, rich, and tannic wines that are expensive and intended for long aging. In the under-$10 category, Cabernets tend to be less tannic and ready for drinking sooner, though some in the $10 to $12 range will age seven to ten years. Of some 750 wineries in California, probably 75 to 80 percent make Cabernet Sauvignon, and there is enormous variation in quality and style. Consistently good ones like BV Beau Tour set a high standard, with good Cabernet character, firm structure, and smooth balance. Poorer wines of this category are blended with lesser grapes or made with Cabernet grown in hot, less desirable regions; they can be green, vegetal, or harsh. The list of good Cabernets, however, is fairly long. New ones continually come along, including attractive ones from Texas, Virginia, and Washington.

Age: **Best at 3–4 years, some will age 5–8 or longer**
Price: **$7–10**
Recommended Producers:

Bandiera ✪	Bel Arbors
Benziger	Big Horn

Bonterra
BV Beau Tour ✪
BV Rutherford ◆
Davis Bynum
Canyon Road
Castoro
Chateau Ste. Michelle
Columbia Crest
Corbett Canyon
Dunnewood
Domaine St. George
Estancia ✪
Fall Creek
Fetzer Barrel Select ✪
Field Stone
Forest Glen ✪
Hawk Crest ✳
Hess Select
Innisfree
Maddalena
Meridian Paso Robles
Louis M. Martini
Mill Creek
The Monterey
  Vineyard ✳
Robert Mondavi
  Coastal
Montdomaine
Napa Ridge
Poppy Hill
Rabbit Ridge
Raymond Amberhill
Round Hill
Saddleback Cellars
St. Supéry ◆
Villa Mt. Eden Cellar
  Select
Wente Estate

Foods: Beef, lamb, hamburgers, meat stews, pastas
  with meat sauce, cheeses mild and savory

Chardonnay

Chardonnay is America's top white grape, widely
produced in styles that run the gamut from
simple, fresh, unoaked versions to rich, oaky,
powerful ones. There are some delightful inexpensive Chardonnays—lively, well balanced, and
flavorful. As the $12-and-under category has ex-
ploded, however, competition is keen and better
quality is often the result. New names constantly
appear, and some very good wines can be had
for $9 to $12—and a fair number for even less.

Since styles vary a bit, I have used a couple of
symbols that give a clue: ♥ indicates perceptible
sweetness (but balanced with good, crisp acidity); ■ represents little or no oak in the wine.

Otherwise, these are perceptibly dry, with moderate oak.

Age: 1–2 years
Price: $6–10
Recommended Producers:

Acacia Caviste
Alderbrook
Alexander Valley
    Vineyards ♦
Argyle
Armida
Bandiera Carneros
Barboursville
Bedell
Belvedere
Benziger
Bonterra
Bon Verre
BV Carneros ♦
Davis Bynum
Callaway Calla-Lees ♥■
Canyon Road
Chateau Ste. Michelle
Chateau Souverain
Christophe ■
Clos du Val Le Clos
Corbett Canyon
    Reserve
Creston
Domaine St. George
Dry Creek
Dunewood
Estancia ✪
Fetzer Barrel Select ♦
Firestone
Forest Glen
Grove Street ♥

Hawk Crest
Hess Select ✪ ■
Jekel Gravelstone
Kendall-Jackson ♥
    Vintner's Reserve
Kunde ♦
La Crema
Leeward
Llano Estacado ■♥
Meridian
Mill Creek
Robert Mondavi
    Coastal
Montdomaine
Monticello
Mountain View
The Monterey
    Vineyard
Oakencroft
Parducci ■
Piedmont
Purple Mountain
Round Hill ■
Schug
Seghesio ✪
Taft Street ♥■
Trefethen Eshcol ✪
Wente Bros.
Hermann Wiemer
Williamsburg Acte 12
Zaca Mesa

Foods: Hard to match because styles differ; sweeter
Chardonnays can handle chicken salad and other
cold meats; drier ones with shellfish (especially
shrimp), pastas with cream sauce, vegetables, or
seafood; either can serve as aperitifs or
summer-afternoon sippers.

Chenin Blanc

Chenin Blanc is the grape that makes Vouvray
and the excellent Savennières in the Loire Valley. California Chenin rarely achieves the character found in the best of those wines, but several
producers are making good, fresh, stylish wines.
A good many others, however, are merely insipid. Two styles exist, dry or slightly off-dry,
and lightly sweet, the latter redeemed by good
acidity that makes for liveliness. Both are best
when young and fresh, but we list them separately.

Age: 1–2 years
Price: $6.50–9.50
Recommended Producers:
Dry. Alexander Valley Vineyards, Chapellet ✪, Folie
à Deux, Daniel Gehrs, Girard, Hogue, Kenwood,
Pedroncelli, Preston ✪, Sullivan, Ventana
Lightly Sweet. Callaway, Cap Rock ✪, Dry Creek,
Fall Creek, Fetzer, Grand Cru, Robert Mondavi,
Parducci, Pine Ridge, Simi, Stevenot, Weibel
Foods: Dry with light fish, white meat chicken;
sweet with chicken salad, ham, liver pâté

Gamay, Gamay Beaujolais

Can America make a light, fruity red with the charm of good Beaujolais? Some producers are trying mightily, with round, fruity, quaffable wines that are proving popular. Some vintners haven't mastered the techniques, however; less good versions can be thin and rather mean. The good ones, like Beaujolais, are best within a year or so of the vintage, and more appealing if they are lightly chilled. The list below includes *nouveau*.

Age: 6–18 months, maybe 2 years
Price: $5–8.50
Recommended Producers: Beringer, BV Beau Tour, Castoro, Fetzer, Geyser Peak ✪, J. Lohr, Louis M. Martini, The Monterey Vineyard, Robert Pecota, Pepperwood Grove, Preston ✳, Weinstock ✳
Foods: Hamburgers, pizza, fried chicken, sausage, cold meats

Gewurztraminer

California Gewurztraminer is usually sweet, with a hint of spiciness in aroma and flavor. Even those labeled Dry tend to be off-dry, not bone-dry like their counterparts in Alsace. When acidity is high and the wines are crisp and lively, they are delightful to drink and can be enjoyed on their own or with food, especially rich Oriental dishes that are deep-fried and some Thai dishes.

Age: 1–3 years
Price: $6.50–10
Recommended Producers: Alexander Valley

Vineyards, Bargetto (dry), Beringer, Chateau St.
Jean, Claiborne & Churchill, Clos du Bois Early
Harvest (dry), Davis Bynum, De Loach, Evesham
Wood, Fetzer, Field Stone, Firestone,
Gundlach-Bundschu (dry), Handley, Husch,
Knudsen-Erath, Lazy Creek, Llano Estacado,
Mark West, Navarro ✪, Palmer, Pedroncelli,
Joseph Phelps, Round Hill, St. Francis, Wente
(dry), Z'Moor

Foods: Spicy and deep-fried Oriental foods, spicy
chicken salad, fresh fruit or fruit salads; by itself

Merlot

Well-made Merlot no longer takes a backseat to
Cabernet as one of California's best reds—it sits
right there on the front seat. Some Merlots are
as tough and firm as Cabernet when they're
young, but the less expensive ones often accentu-
ate the grape's soft, plummy fruit and alluring
texture. They're mostly ready to drink when you
buy them, and often your best match with lamb.
If you buy one that seems a little tight, decant it
out of and back into the bottle, which should
aerate it enough to soften it. Very good Merlot is
available for under $10, and outstanding ones
for a few dollars more.

Age: Drinkable at 2 years, best at 3–4, can hold 5–7
Price: $7.50–12
Recommended Producers: BV Beau Tour, Buena
   Vista, Covey Run, Creston, Cypress, Dunnewood,
   Estancia, Firestone, Forest Glen, Hogue, Geyser
   Peak, Glen Ellen, Guenoc, Lakespring, Louis M.
   Martini, Meadow Glen, Monterey Vineyard
   Classic, Mt. Konocti, Mountain View, Napa Ridge,
   Palmer, Sebastiani, Stone Creek, Trentadue

Foods: Lamb, roast beef, steak, duck, goose, rabbit, grilled tuna

Muscat, Malvasia

Good Muscat, with its lightly spicy, faintly exotic flavors, is becoming more popular, happily. It is lightly sweet unless the label says Late Harvest. My hope is that someone takes up the challenge to produce a fine *dry* Muscat that isn't bitter— hard to do, so it may be a while. Meanwhile, there are some charming Muscats, and Bonny Doon's delightful Malvasia, to sip on a late sunny afternoon, or to enjoy with a ripe peach.

Age: 1 year
Price: $7–8
Recommended Producers: Alderbrook, Benziger, Bonny Doon Ca' del Solo, Eberle, Folie à Deux, Lava Cap, Markham, Monte Volpe, Fess Parker, Quady Electra
Foods: Peaches, pears, papayas, strawberries; by itself

Petite Sirah, Syrah

Petite Sirah is an old variety in California, originally thought to be the Syrah of the Rhône Valley. Then it was thought to be a lesser variety known there as the Durif, used primarily for blending. Its origin is still somewhat moot. Petite Sirah was once widely planted in warmer regions and used to beef up jug wines, but a few producers produce dark, hefty, richly textured reds from it that have flavors of black raspberries and some of the peppery character of Rhône reds.

Syrah is the genuine Rhône variety used to make some of the Rhône Valley's most distinguished reds, such as Hermitage, Côte Rotie, and Cornas, Syrah is still fairly new to California, but it's hot because several innovative winemakers have produced some dramatic reds with it. Limited in quantity, most Syrahs cost well over $12; those that don't tend to be lighter in character and pizzazz. Those included here are listed with the Petite Sirahs, but Syrah follows the winery name.

Age: 3–5 years, will age

Price: $5.50–9

Recommended Producers: Bogle, Concannon, Edmunds St. John Syrah, Foppiano, Guenoc, Louis M. Martini ✪, McDowell Les Vieux Cépages, Mirassou, Parducci, Qupé Syrah, Trentadue, Zaca Mesa Syrah

Foods: Grilled steak, braised brisket, meat or game stews, savory cheeses like aged Cheddar, Parmesan, or Asiago, dry Jack; also goat and blue cheeses

Pinot Blanc

A firm, medium-bodied, dry white, often described as a leaner Chardonnay. Fruity and lightly oaked (occasionally barrel-fermented), Pinot Blanc is a good alternative to Chardonnay —though some barrel-fermented ones are fairly pricey now. There aren't many Pinot Blancs, but some new planting is under way, so we may see more.

Age: 1–2 years, can stretch

Price: $8–12

Recommended Producers: Buehler, Chateau St.
   Jean, Congress Springs, Daniel Gehrs, Jekel,
   Lockwood, Mirassou White Burgundy (mostly
   Pinot Blanc), Monte Volpe, Palmer, Panther
   Creek Melon, Saddleback Cellars

Pinot Gris

Pinot Gris was practically unknown in this country a decade ago. This stylish white, crisp and
dry with slightly steely fruit, has gained a following in recent years, and a well-deserved one for
its delightful fresh flavor. Most currently come
from Oregon, the first region to focus on Pinot
Gris in the United States. Wider planting is
under way in the Willamette Valley, as well as in
other states such as Virginia and California. A
few are labeled with the Italian name, Pinot
Grigio.

Age: 1–3 years
Price: $8.99–12
Recommended Producers: Adelsheim,
   Barboursville, Elk Cove, King Estate,
   Knudsen-Erath, Montinore, Navarro, Oak Knoll,
   Red Hawk, Rex Hill, Simeon ♦, Ivan Tamas,
   Yamhill Valley
Foods: Fish, especially salmon, seafood pastas,
   appetizers, pâté

Pinot Noir

California is producing outstanding Pinot Noirs
these days, the best of them fairly pricey. Good
ones under $10 tend to be lighter, fruitier, acces-
sible at a younger age, and quite versatile with a

broad range of foods. If they are quite light, the flavor may be enhanced by slight chilling, but it isn't necessarily color that tells you that. Some of the cherry-colored Pinots have quite intense flavor, without the tannin of their more exalted brothers.

Age: 2–4 years
Price: $6–12
Recommended Producers:

Alexander Valley
   Vineyards
Argyle
Armida
Arterberry
Benton Lane
Bethel Heights First
   Release
BV Carneros ♦
Davis Bynum
Christophe Carneros
Congress Springs ♦
Creston
Duck Pond ✳
Dunnewood
Estancia
Eyrie Special Selection
Fleur de Carneros
Hargrave
Iron Horse Cuvée 'R'
King's Ridge
Knudsen-Erath
La Crema
Louis M. Martini
Meridian
Mont St. John
The Monterey
   Vineyard
Mountain View ✪
Napa Ridge ✪
Oak Knoll
Panther Creek
Pepperwood Springs
Santa Barbara Winery
Saintsbury Garnet ✪
Seghesio ✪
Sokol-Blosser
Steele Shooting Star
Weinstock Reserve

Foods: Grilled or roast chicken, duck, grilled salmon, roast pork, country pâtés, mild cheeses like Port Salut, Monterey Jack, goat

Pinot Noir Blanc

If you take red grapes and drain off the free-run juice or press it lightly, you'll get wines with a light blush color—deeper, if more time with the grape skin is allowed, since that is where the color pigments are. These can be delightful wines when well made, perfect for sipping or for weekend brunches or picnics. They should be quite crisp and not too sweet, like those recommended below. Most pink wines today are made from Zinfandel, but a few very good ones are still made from Pinot Noir. They can sure cool down a chili-lacerated palate.

Age: 6–18 months
Price: $4–8
Recommended Producers: Caymus Oeil de Perdrix,
    Hagafen, Leeward Coral, Palmer,
    Schwartzenberg
Foods: Ham, cold cuts, cold chicken or turkey,
    chicken salad, goat-cheese salad, spicy Mexican

Proprietary Reds

These blended reds are given simple names like Red Table Wine or Vintage White, sometimes proprietary names like Trefethen's Eshcol or Boeger's whimsical Hangtown Red. They are usually made from surplus varieties, often grown on the estate, and can be excellent value for everyday drinking—or even a bit better than that. Most are light or medium-bodied, but some, like Marty Griffin's Big Red, are robust and meaty. Other good ones pop up from time to time, but the ones listed here are consistently good. Some come in 1.5-liter magnums, a convenient size for large gatherings.

Age: Often nonvintage, always ready for immediate
    drinking

Price: $4–7.50

Recommended Producers: Big House Red, Boeger Hangtown Red, Bonny Doon, Canoe Ridge Red Table, Fetzer Premium Red, Marty Griffin's Big Red, Gundlach-Bundschu Sonoma Red, Heitz Ryan's Red, Le Clos Red, The Monterey Vineyard Classic Red, Peachy Canyon Incredible Red, Pedroncelli Sonoma Red, R. H. Phillips Night Harvest Cuvée Rouge ✪, Preston Estate Red, Raymond, Trefethen Eshcol Cabernet/Merlot ✪, Trentadue Red

Foods: Hamburgers to grilled steak

Rhône Style/Blends

Red Rhône varieties such as Syrah, Mourvèdre, Grenache and Cinsaut are expanding in vineyards throughout California and elsewhere (Virginia, Washington). Most varietals—wines named for a single grape—are usually over $12 because production is limited, though a few fall within our price limit. More prevalent are Rhône-style blends, which can be quite charming and versatile with food, from goat cheese to grilled meats and vegetables, Mediterranean pastas and pizza. *Recommended:* Bonny Doon Clos de Gilroy ✪ & Le Gaucher, Cline Carignane & Oakley Cuvee, Edmunds St. John New World Red, McDowell Bistro Rouge, Pellegrini Old Vines Carignane, Phelps Vin du Mistral Rouge, R. H. Phillips Alliance & Mourvèdre, Preston Faux ✪, Quivira Dry Creek Cuvée, Rabbit Ridge Allure ✪, Trentadue Old Patch Red, Zaca Mesa

Riesling (Johannisberg or White)

Riesling is such a hard sell in the United States that many Riesling vineyards have been grafted over to other varieties, mostly Chardonnay (the easy sell). Some of the best producers are still at it, happily, producing some very charming wines. The true German Riesling is called Johannisberg or White Riesling in America to distinguish it from lesser Riesling varieties (like Franken Riesling or Monterey Riesling, which are actually Sylvaner). Styles of Riesling range from off-dry to lightly sweet to very sweet late-harvest and Botrytised wines. Though the grape does not achieve the depth and complexity that it does at the great estates of the Rhine and Mosel valleys in Germany, there are a number of lovely, fragrant, flowery Rieslings made here, and truly luscious late-harvest ones. Light Rieslings are never more than $10, and most are well under that. However, only a few of the late-harvest wines—that I can recommend, at any rate—fall within our limits. Many of these wines come in half-bottles. Rieslings are charming when they are young and fresh, but well-balanced ones, dry or sweet, will keep several years if properly stored in cool conditions. I once tasted a ten-year-old Chappellet Dry Riesling that was as crisp and fresh as a two-year-old one, and much more interesting. Like many wineries, Chappellet stopped making Riesling some years ago.

Wines labeled Dry Riesling are rarely completely dry here, but high acidity in the good ones makes them seem quite dry. For clarity, I've separated the three most popular styles in our price range as follows: Dry, Lightly Sweet, and Late Harvest.

Age: 1–3 years, Late Harvest can last 5–8 or more
   depending on balance
Price: $6–10

Dry, Off-dry: Bonny Doon, Chateau Ste. Michelle ❍,
   Clos du Bois, Firestone, Greenwood Ridge ❍,
   Hogue, Jekel, Mt. Konocti, Joseph Phelps,
   Rapidan River, Renaissance, Trefethen, Van
   Duzer, Hermann Wiemer
Foods: Chicken, chicken salad, Oriental foods, light
   fish such as sea bass, trout, pike; smoked salmon;
   good aperitif
Lightly Sweet: Babcock, Fetzer ❍, Elk Cove,
   Firestone ❍, Dr. K. Frank, Freemark Abbey,
   Glenora, Grgich Hills, Haywood, Hidden Cellars,
   Hogue, Jekel ❍, Kendall-Jackson, Llano Estacado,
   Louis M. Martini, Robert Mondavi, Obester,
   Parducci, Rapidan River, St. Francis,
   Smith-Madrone, Sokol-Blosser, Wagner, Wente,
   Zaca Mesa
Foods: Delightful on their own, with fresh fruit or
   light desserts; foods with sweet sauces
Late Harvest: Arciero, Franciscan, Hogue,
   Kendall-Jackson, Pedroncelli, Renaissance
Foods: Fruit desserts, particularly those made with
   peaches or apricots; can also serve *as* dessert,
   with light cake or cookies

Rosés

Rosés are slightly out of favor with the advance-
ment of the popular blush, White Zinfandel. Generic rosés can be vapid and feeble. If you want
rosé, varietal rosés, those made from a single
variety such as Zinfandel or Cabernet Sauvignon,
are the only way to go. I don't have many to
recommend, but they are the best of the breed.
Most are lightly sweet (the Firestone is the driest) but well balanced and crisp. See also Vin
Gris, the best pinks today.

Age: 1–2 years
Price: $5–7.50
Recommended Producers: Cline Angel Rosé,
    Firestone Rosé of Cabernet Sauvignon, Heitz
    Grignolino Rosé, Mirassou Petite Rosé, Robert
    Mondavi Woodbridge Gamay Rosé, Monte Volpe
    Nebbiolo, Pedroncelli Zinfandel Rosé, Simi Rosé
    of Cabernet Sauvignon
Foods: Barbecues, picnics, Tex-Mex, dishes laced
    with chilis

Sauvignon Blanc (also labeled Fumé Blanc)

The runner-up in white wines, a close second to
inexpensive Chardonnays—and often surpassing
them for my money. Dry, crisp, made with much
greater finesse than formerly, Sauvignon Blancs
represent some of the best values in California
white wine. You never have to lay out more than
$10 to get good, even excellent, Sauvignon Blanc
—despite the fact that some of the front-runners
have become pretty pricey. It's not that they
aren't worth it, it's just that there are so many
good ones for less. It's the largest single category, in fact. The names Sauvignon Blanc and
Fumé Blanc are used at the whim of the winery
and are not a useful clue to style.

Styles do vary. Some are simple, made in
a Loire-like style with no oak influence. More
and more Sauvignons, however, are barrel-
fermented or aged for a time in oak, which adds
an extra dimension. Semillon is sometimes
blended with them. Styles from a given winery
may change from one year to the next—no oak in
one vintage, then a switch to oak aging or barrel
fermentation the next. Most are dry, but some

have residual sugar—I include only the well-made ones that are well balanced with acidity. Perceptible sweetness is indicated by the symbol ♥. The term Fumé is included when the wine is so labeled; otherwise the label reads Sauvignon Blanc. Some wineries produce both, so the one that is recommended is indicated.

Age: 1–2 years, some go 3 or 4
Price: $7–10
Recommended Producers:

Adler Fels
Alderbrook
Arbor Crest ♥
Barnard Griffin
Benziger Fumé
Beringer Knight's
  Valley Fumé
Bernardus
Brander ✪
Cap Rock ♥
Carey
Caymus
Chalk Hill
Château St. Jean
  Sonoma Fumé ♥
Concannon
DeLoach Fumé ✳
Dry Creek Fumé ✳
Estancia ✪
Fall Creek
Ferrari-Carano ♥✳
Foppiano
J. Fritz ✳
Gallo ♥
Greenwood Ridge
Groth
Hanna

Havens
Hawk Crest
Louis Honig
Husch ♥
Iron Horse Fumé ✳
Kendall-Jackson ♥
Kenwood
Llano Estacado
Lockwood ✳
Markham
Mayacamas
Robert Mondavi Fumé
Mt. Konocti Fumé
The Monterey
  Vineyard
Morgan
Murphy-Goode Fumé
Pedroncelli Fumé
Robert Pepi
R. H. Phillips
Preston Cuvée de
  Fumé ✳
Quivira
Round Hill Fumé
Sanford
Silverado ✳
Simi

Rodney Strong	Stonegate
Charlotte's Home	Wildhurst
Vyd ✳	William Hill

Vin Gris

I'm greatly in hopes this category will grow. Essentially, *vin gris* is a pale, *dry* rosé or blush wine made from red grapes. There are only a few made in California, hardly what you would call a category. American consumers are unfamiliar with the concept, expecting pink wines always to be sweet. Sanford Winery made an excellent dry *vin gris* from Pinot Noir for several years, then stopped because it didn't sell. I'm glad to report that as of 1989 Richard Sanford is making it again in small quantities. The popularity of Bonny Doon's Vin Gris de Cigare (a blend of Rhône varieties) is helping. I've urged Au Bon Climat to have a go at *vin gris*—as long as they keep it under $10. Maybe others will follow suit. The important thing is that it be *dry;* otherwise it is not a true *vin gris.*

Age: 1–2 years, sometimes 3
Price: $7–9
Recommended Producers: Bonny Doon Vin Gris de Cigare ✪, Calera, Edmunds St. John, Edna Valley, Ojai, Saintsbury Vin Gris, Sanford ✪
Foods: Grilled sausage, prosciutto, roast ham or pork, cold chicken, smoked turkey, duck, goat cheese; alone, as an aperitif, or with snacks

Zinfandel

The most American of reds, generally robustly fruity, with flavors reminiscent of raspberries or huckleberries. Some versions are fairly tannic, with chewy textures, but the tannic monsters of yore have largely disappeared and certainly are not recommended here. In fact, the bulk of Zinfandel grapes now go to make white Zinfandel, diverting a lot of the mediocre wine that used to be made by the tankful. The best practitioners of Zinfandel continue to make rich, wonderful reds that are excellent value, with a number of Superbuys! Many good ones are priced at $12 and under. Some of the most sought after are made in limited quantities and can command more; often they are worth it, though they are sometimes found for less at discount stores. Zinfandel is prized for its appealing thrust of fruit, showiest in its first few years. But well-balanced Zinfandels (under 13.5 percent alcohol) can age a decade or more, becoming rather Cabernet-like with age.

Age: **Often drinkable at 2 years, but richer ones at 3–5; well-balanced Zins can age a decade or longer**

Price: **$7–10 +**

Recommended Producers:

Alderbrook	Louis M. Martini ✪
Belvedere	Meeker ✳
Benziger	Peachy Canyon
Buehler	Pedroncelli
Burgess	Preston
Davis Bynum	Quivira
Castoro ✪	Rabbit Ridge ✳
Château Souverain	A Rafanelli ✪
Cline	Ravenswood Vintner's
Foppiano	Blend
J. Fritz	Ridge Paso Robles ✳♦
Franciscan Hop Kiln	Ridge Sonoma ✳
Kendall-Jackson	Rosenblum
Lamborn Family ♦	Sausal

Steele Shooting Star	V. Sattui
Sutter Home Reserve	Villa Mt. Eden
Swanson	Wildhurst

White Zinfandel

Just because most white Zinfandel is sweet and
insipid doesn't mean there aren't truly charming
ones that are only lightly sweet, crisp, lively, and
well balanced. These I can recommend happily
for casual sipping.

Age: 6–18 months
Price: $5–6.50
Recommended Producers: Bandiera, Beringer,
   Buehler, DeLoach ✳, Kenwood, Louis M. Martini
   ✳, Mirassou, Robert Mondavi Woodbridge ✳,
   The Monterey Vineyard, Mountain View,
   Pedroncelli, Stevenot, Ivan Tamas, Weinstock

Other U.S. Wines

Wines from other parts of the United States are
steadily improving. Some, indeed, have arrived,
especially those of the Northwest, which is producing wines that can rival many of the best from
California (Riesling, Sauvignon Blanc, Cabernet,
Pinot Noir). Washington and Oregon wines are
also gaining wider distribution around the country. The same is true for New York, where the
small wineries have effected a dramatic revolu-
tion in quality and style. Texas and Virginia are
also growing rapidly and producing excellent
wines. Wines with good distribution are also included in appropriate categories.

Many of the best regional wines have escalated in price as their quality has gained recognition. However, those that fall within our price range are well worth seeking out if you find yourself in their immediate areas.

Arkansas. Wiederkehr Cabernet Sauvignon,
Vidal, Johannisberg Riesling
Colorado. Plum Creek Cellars Merlot,
Chardonnay
Connecticut. Crosswoods Scrimshaw White,
Chardonnay
Chambord Chardonnay
Idaho. Ste. Chapelle Riesling, Brut
Maryland. Catoctin Chardonnay, Mariage Byrd
Merlot
Michigan. Château Grand Traverse Riesling
Fenn Valley Chancellor
Missouri. Les Bourgeois Vidal
Hermannhof Vignole
Mt. Pleasant Vidal, Vintage Port
Montelle Norton
Stone Hill Norton, Vignole
New Jersey. Alba Riesling, Vidal Reserve
Tewksberry Gewurztraminer
New Mexico. Gruet Brut
Las Nutrias Pinot Noir
New York. Bedell Cabernet Sauvignon,
Chardonnay
Glenora Chardonnay, Riesling
Great Western Ice Wine
Hargrave Petite Chardonnay, Petite
Cabernet, Blanc de Pinot Noir
Hermann Wiemer Dry Riesling, Pinot Noir
Konstantin Frank Johannisberg Riesling
Lamoreaux Landing Riesling, Chardonnay
Millbrook Chardonnay, Pinot Noir, Merlot
Palmer Chardonnay, Merlot

Pindar Merlot
Swedish Hill Riesling
Wagner Seyval Blanc, Ravat Ice Wine
West Park Chardonnay
North Carolina. Biltmore Pinot Noir, Blanc de
   Blancs
West Bend Chardonnay, Sauvignon Blanc
Ohio. Chalet Debonné, Firelands, Markko
Pennsylvania. Chaddsford Spring Wine,
   Nouveau
Rhode Island. Sakonnet Chardonnay, Vidal
   Blanc
Texas. Homestead Cabernet Sauvignon
   Llano Estacado Gewurztraminer, Riesling
   Slaughter-Leftwych Sauvignon Blanc, Austin
   Blush
Virginia. Ingleside Plantation Chesapeake
      White, Blanc de Blancs, Cabernet
      Sauvignon
   Meredyth Seyval Blanc, Chardonnay
   Oakencroft Countryside White
   Prince Michel Blanc de Noir, Chardonnay
Washington. Columbia Sémillon, Merlot,
      Johannisberg Riesling
   Lemberger
   Pacifica Dry White
   Salishan Dry Riesling
   Tagaris Pinot Noir
   White Heron Pinot Noir
West Virginia. Robert Pliska Foch
Wisconsin. Wollersheim Reserve Red

SUPERBUYS / UNITED STATES

White/Pink
Bonny Doon Vin Gris, $8.99
Brander Sauvignon Blanc, $9

Cap Rock Chenin Blanc, $7
Chappellet Chenin Blanc, $7.29
Chateau Ste. Michelle Dry Riesling, $5.99
Corbett Canyon Chardonnay Reserve, $9.50
Estancia Chardonnay, $10
Estancia Sauvignon Blanc, $8
Fetzer Johannisberg Riesling, $6.75
Firestone Johannisberg Riesling, $9
Hess Select Chardonnay, $9.99
Jekel Johannisberg Riesling, $7.99
Knudsen-Erath Pinot Gris, $10
Robert Mondavi Fumé Blanc, $9
Navarro Gewurztraminer, $7
Sanford Vin Gris, $9
Seghesio Chardonnay, $7.99
Trefethen Eshcol Chardonnay, $7–10

Red

Bandiera Cabernet Sauvignon, $6.99
Bonny Doon Clos de Gilroy, $8.99
BV Beau Tour Cabernet Sauvignon, $7–9
Castoro Zinfandel, $7–9
Estancia Cabernet Sauvignon, $9
Geyser Peak Gamay Beaujolais, $8
Louis M. Martini Petite Sirah, $10
Louis M. Martini Zinfandel, $8.50
Napa Ridge Pinot Noir, $6–7
R. H. Phillips Night Harvest Cuvée Rouge, $5
Preston Faux, $8–10
Rabbit Ridge Allure, $9
A. Rafanelli Zinfandel, $10
Saintsbury Garnet Pinot Noir, $10
Seghesio Pinot Noir, $9–11
Stone Creek Merlot, $6

Latin America

Latin American wines are apt to emerge impressively during this decade. Chile has already made a big splash, producing sensational values in red wines (watch for Superbuys). Indeed, they compete favorably with red wines made anywhere now. Chile makes some remarkably flavorful and well-balanced Cabernet Sauvignon, Bordeaux-like in structure and style. This is not mere coincidence. When the terrible phylloxera (a bug that eats vine roots) devastated the vineyards of Bordeaux in the 1880s, several Bordeaux vintners came to Chile to make wine, establishing a style with Cabernet that is still followed today. Interest from Bordeaux also continues. Consulting enologist Emile Peynaud has lent his expertise to Chilean winemakers. The owners of Châteaux Lafite-Rothschild have invested in vineyards there, producing wine under the Los

Vascos label. Several California vintners are also importing Chilean varietals.

Chilean Cabernets tend to be drinkable early but often have amazing capacity for aging. The climate and soils of Chile's inland valleys give the wines their edge in character and quality. In recent years, good Chardonnay, Merlot, and Sauvignon Blanc have also begun to appear. A problem for Chile is that, because the wines are so reasonable, many people have jumped on the bandwagon to bring in Chilean wines. Individuals go down from California, for instance, and buy up available wine, slap a label on it, and import it, hoping it will become a hot new property. Those who produce the best wines, though, are mostly well-established producers who have good vineyards, or newcomers who have bought or planted vineyards in the better regions. Chile is hot, and getting hotter.

The same cannot be said for Argentina. This country's wine potential has never been properly realized, merely exploited to produce as much quantity as possible with little regard to quality. Argentina is a sleeping giant, however; it could do more and better—if only Argentine vintners would begin to produce wines from lower yields with more concentration. The Argentine wine industry hasn't the global outlook that Chile has and seems to have little sense of international standards. They produce as much as possible from every vineyard, extracting high yields that dilute character and make for mediocre quality. They age the wines in huge old wooden vats that do little to improve them (in fact, they may have the opposite effect) or in large stainless steel vats that contribute nothing to flavor—which would be all right except there is so little in the first place.

There are a few producers who do a good job, but by far the largest number are interested in quantity over quality. Argentine wines are grown on broad, flat plateaus in the northwestern part of the country at the foot of the Andes. The vines are grafted because phylloxera came in the late nineteenth century (The little bug did not cross the Andes, however, so Chilean vines grow on their own roots, accounting for some of the rather aggressive character when the vines are young.) Argentina is the fifth-largest producer of wine in the world and third in per capita consumption. Most of the wine stays in Argentina or goes elsewhere in South America. If Argentina ever awakes to what is possible, we may see excellent values here. As it is, I have only a few labels to recommend.

Mexico is another area of great potential, but here too they need to get their act together. At the moment the largest area for serious grape growing is in Baja California, but vineyards in the central highlands have produced good Cabernet Sauvignon and other reds (including Zinfandel), as well as Chardonnay and Pinot Noir that offer positive hope for the future. Mexican wines got a boost when a Domecq Cabernet won recognition in the Paris Olympiad held by Gault-Millau.

Brazil and Uruguay also produce wine and might possibly do well if the industry concentrates on clean, well-balanced wines. At the moment almost nothing is available here except the Marcus James label from Brazil, producing decent if unremarkable white Zinfandel and other inexpensive varietals.

CHILE

We would have been drinking the fine wines of
Chile far sooner had it not been for a political
climate that interfered with exports. Since the
early 1980s, however, the wines have flowed
north in greater number, and Americans have
been pleased by the values they offer, particularly in red wines.

Chile's wine regions are in the inland valleys
north and south of Santiago. Aconcagua is to the
north, Maipo in the south with its subdistricts of
Maule, Mataquito, Curicó, and Lontué. Though
you will see such names on labels, at this stage
the best guide to quality is the producer name.

In view of the growing quality and reputation
of Chilean wines, we can expect to see prices
rise for the better and more sought-after wines.
It is rather amazing that one can purchase outstanding Cabernet Sauvignon such as the Cousiño Macul for as little as $6, and well under $10
for the Reserva. At their best, these wines are
brimming with berryish fruit and cedary flavors
typical of fine Cabernet, but the good ones are
never heavy or overripe.

Because of fine balance and medium body,
Chilean Cabernet is remarkably versatile with
food, from barbecued meats to roast chicken,
lamb, or beef, as well as veal and light game, and
savory cheese. Vintages are fairly even in Chile;
poor vintages are rare; poorly made wines, however, are not so rare, a situation also likely to
improve.

Chile now produces several other varietals,
such as Merlot, and Pinot Noir in reds, Chardonnay, Riesling, Sauvignon Blanc, and Sémillon in
whites. Sauvignon Blanc, dry, crisp, and rather

steely, is the most successful other than Cabernet at the moment. The others I would rate average to good, but future prospects as the vines mature and winemakers gain experience with Chardonnay, Merlot, and Pinot Noir look bright.

Best Wine:
  Cabernet Sauvignon
Next:
  Sauvignon Blanc
  Merlot
  Chardonnay

Cabernet Sauvignon

There are some sensational values here, and the better properties rarely miss, though on occasion a few of the regular Cabernets (non-Reservas) taste a little thin. Cousiño Macul, for instance, consistently scores with simple Cabernet, but the 1986 was exaggeratedly vegetal—perhaps due to wines from young vines. The Santa Rita 120, on the other hand, is quite jammy, somewhat on the mellow side, while Concha y Toro Cabernets tend to be coarse and rustic. The best values by far are the Reservas. These are better lots of wine that are aged longer and have the most flavor and depth. Cousiño Macul's Antiguas Reserva is outstanding, as are the Reservas of Santa Rita, Errazuriz Panquehue, and Concha y Toro Casillero del Diablo. These wines, smooth and ready to drink when you buy them, nevertheless have the balance and depth to age further, easily to eight or ten years. New labels are rapidly appearing from Chile, some good, some not.

Age: 2–4 years; Reservas 4–6, may go 8–10 or more
Price: $4.50–6; Reservas $6–10
Recommended Producers: Caliterra ✪, Canepa
    Finisimo, Casillero del Diablo, Cousiño Macul
    (Antiguas Reserva) ✳, Errazuriz, Saint Morillon,
    Santa Carolina (Reserva ✪), Santa Rita Medalla
    Real ✪, Miguel Torres, Undurraga, Los Vascos ✪
Foods: Reservas are excellent with lamb or beef,
    grilled or roasted; non-Reservas with lighter fare,
    like hamburgers, grilled chicken, veal stew

Chardonnay

Chile is just getting started with Chardonnay,
and plantings are expanding rapidly. Some of
the wines are fresh and attractive but don't have
much character yet; that should come as the
vines mature. While at the moment Sauvignon
Blanc is a better buy, I believe the Chardonnays
of Chile will come into their own, and they bear
watching. Don't look for rich, oaky styles yet
(which will likely cost more anyway)—the wines
are dry, fruity, simple but increasingly appealing. Chardonnay grapes seem to cost more
everywhere, and prices for some Chilean Chardonnay are at the upper end of the scale.

Age: 1–3 years
Price: $5–8
Recommended Producers: Caliterra ✳, Casillero del
    Diablo, Cousiño Macul, Santa Rita Reserva,
    Miguel Torres, Valdivieso, Los Vascos
Foods: Simply prepared fish, cold shrimp, chicken
    (white meat), smoked turkey

Merlot

Not as widely planted as Cabernet Sauvignon, and the wines are not as impressive as yet. More vineyards are being planted, and there is every reason to expect Merlot to do well in Chile as winemakers become more experienced with the variety. Good ones have plummy, berryish fruit, but some of the wines have a vegetal accent that should be toned down (or, one hopes, eliminated altogether); others seem overchaptalized (sugar added before fermentation to add body)—hence, the few recommendations that appear here.

Age: 2–4 years
Price: $4–7
Recommended Producers: Los Boldos, Concha y
    Toro, Errazuriz, Santa Rita, Sergio Traverso ✪
Foods: Burgers, pork chops, quiche, and other
    cheese dishes

Sauvignon Blanc

Chilean winemakers are old hands with Sauvignon Blanc, and it is their finest white wine at the moment. Top ones are dry, crisp, and snappy, though sometimes the tartness and sharp angularity of young Sauvignons bites a bit (especially in those for under $4.50). Reservas have more flavor and better balance. Los Vascos makes one of the cleanest, smoothest, and most appealing Sauvignons—an excellent example of what can be done when the grapes are balanced and the winemaking is skilled and conscientious.

Age: 1–3 years
Price: $4.50–7

Recommended Producers: Los Boldos, Caliterra ✱,
   Casa Lapostelle, Cousiño Macul, Errazuriz ✱,
   Marqués de Casa, Saint Morillon, Santa Rita
   Reserva, Miguel Torres ✱, Sergio Traverso, Los
   Vascos Reserva ✪
Foods: Shellfish, swordfish, shark, seafood pastas,
   roasted red peppers with garlic, goat cheese

SUPERBUYS / CHILE

White
   Caliterra Chardonnay, $7
   Los Vascos Sauvignon Blanc, $5.99

Red
   Caliterra Cabernet Sauvignon, $7
   Cousiño Macul Cabernet Sauvignon Antiguas
      Reservas, $7.50−9
   Errazuriz Cabernet Sauvignon, $9
   Santa Carolina Cabernet Reserva, $8
   Santa Rita Medalla Real, $7.49−8
   Sergio Traverso Merlot, $6.99

ARGENTINA

Argentina should be producing good, sturdy,
flavorful reds and crisp stylish whites. Surely
vintners will get the message sometime during
this decade and begin to produce wines that are
worthy of attention, and the consumer's dollar.
Meanwhile, precious little that can meet those
demands is available in the United States. Of
those imported, Cabernet Sauvignon is the best,
but other varietals with promise are Chardonnay
(Navarro Correas), Merlot, Riesling, and Syrah.

Cabernet Sauvignon

Cabernet is often blended with Malbec, a lesser Bordeaux red grape, and some Merlot, though little is grown there as yet. Most Argentine Cabernet is medium weight in terms of body, without much structure or depth, but some of the meatier ones are quite good.

Age: 3–6 years
Price: $6–7
Recommended Producers: Bianchi Particular, Navarro Correas ✳, San Felipe, Pascual Toso, Trapiche
Foods: Steak, roast beef, beef stew, grilled chicken

Chardonnay

There is not a lot of varietal character in Argentine Chardonnays, but they do have freshness and a crisp, stylish appeal that shows what Argentine wineries can do with the grape when they try. The ones recommended are quite reasonable and well worth a try; others may soon surface.

Age: 1–2 years
Price: $5–8
Recommended Producers: Catena ✳, Navarro Correas, San Felipe, Trapiche
Foods: Mild fish or chicken, scallops

Syrah

Syrah could prove to be one of Argentina's finest reds. The climate is highly suitable to this Rhône variety. Most is rather light in style now, but watch for sturdier versions to make their appearance in the next few years.

Age: 2–5 years
Price: $8–10
Recommended Producer: Navarro Correas
Foods: Burgers, chops, grilled sausage

8

Germany

The nineties, I believe, will bring much greater acceptance of German wines—and deservedly. Germany makes some of the most delectable wines available, but for too long they have been *outré*—out, because dry wines are "in" and German wines are sweet. There ought to be room for both styles; they are not exactly interchangeable. With some foods only dry will do, but there are times when off-dry or lightly sweet is perfection. Try a Kabinett Riesling with smoked salmon to see what I mean; Chardonnay just can't handle it. Novice wine drinkers who prefer sweet wines can do no better than hone their palates on fine Rieslings from the Rhine and Mosel valleys.

Most of the people who avoid German Rieslings either have never tasted them or have tasted poor ones. Pour a good one, however, and it isn't hard to win someone over. They are easy wines to like. The worldwide demand for dry wine hurt German wine sales during the eighties. As a result, drier styles of German wine (Trocken and Halbtrocken) have emerged. Some, especially those labeled Halbtrocken Kabinett or Spätlese, are very exciting wines with some outstanding values among them.

Another reason people ignore German wines is that they seem too difficult to understand—those Gothic labels are beautiful but hard to read, and many of the terms are unpronounceable if you don't know German. Don't let that put you off—the wine inside those tall green (Mosel) or brown (Rhine) bottles is light, fruity, friendly, and delicious, frequently compelling in character but never forbidding. I won't try to explain German geography and nomenclature here. There are several current books that do a good job of that, so seek them out if you want to know more.

Here I *am* going to define certain terms to look for on the label and name some of the top estates, producers, and importers of reliable quality with fairly reasonable distribution across the country.

Riesling. This is Germany's finest wine grape, the only grape that consistently produces well in Germany. [Exceptions: Baden, which produces dry and quite good Pinot Blanc (Weissburgunder), and Pinot Gris (Rulander), as well as Riesling.] If the label does not specifically say Riesling, then some other grape variety (Müller-Thurgau, Kerner, Sylvaner) is used, and none compare in character, flavor, or quality. You won't see Riesling on Liebfraumilch; by German law the wine must contain only 51 percent Riesling, and rarely contains more. U.S. law requires 75 percent for the grape to be named.

Trocken, Halbtrocken. Terms mean "dry" or "half-dry." Acidity in German Rieslings is high, so half-dry really comes across as quite dry.

Qualitätswein (QbA). The term means "quality wine," but it's the level for average to good wines.

Prädikat, or Qualitätswein mit Prädikat (QmP). The highest quality level for German wines, those with only natural sweetness. This level is further divided into five levels that indicate degrees of sweetness, as follows:

Kabinett. The driest level of Prädikat wines, but often off-dry or faintly sweet. It can be excellent value at $7 to $9. Kabinett Halbtrocken tends to be firmly dry.

Spätlese. Means "late harvest" and signifies richer wines than Kabinett but still only lightly sweet, especially those labeled Halbtrocken.

Auslese. "Specially selected late harvest," definitely sweet and quite luscious, the grapes often affected by the noble rot *Botrytis cinerea* (*Edelfäule* in German), the same mold that creates Sauternes. The best are too expensive for us, but check out specials or discount stores, which may have them marked down.

Beerenauslese (BA), Trockenbeerenauslese (TBA), and Eiswein. Germany's sweetest nectars, concentrated knockouts but limited in quantity, and very expensive, even in half-bottles.

Prices for Kabinetts and Spätlesen have already begun to rise from the top estates. Until the momentum for fine German wines gathers steam, however, you will find many of them marked down. Listed below are the top producers and estates, as well as shippers or importers who are reliable. It is interesting to note that producers committed to quality usually demonstrate excellent quality at all levels of production, from simple QbA Rieslings to their finest Auslesen.

CAUTION: *Beware* prices of $5 or under unless you personally know the wine and like it, or it is one listed here that's on sale or discounted. Wines of those marked ♦, unfortunately, rarely fall within our price limit, but they can be well worth a few extra dollars.

TOP PRODUCERS

Mosel
Bergweiler-Prüm
J. J. Christoffel
Conrad-Bartz
Deinhard
Dr. Fischer
Friedrich-Wilhelm
　Gymnasium
Willi Haag
von Hovel
Karlsmuhle
von Kesselstatt
Dr. Loosen
Maximin Grünhaus
Merkelbach
Meulenhof
Mönchhof
Moselland

Egon Müller ♦
Pauly-Bergweiler ♦
J. J. Prüm
Max Richter
Willi Schäfer
von Schleinitz
Selbach-Oster
Vereinigte Hospitien
Wegeler-Deinhard
F. Weins-Prüm

Rhine
Balbach Erben
Bassermann-Jordan
von Buhl
Burklin-Wolf
Kurt Darting
H. Dönnhoff (Nahe)

Fischer Erben
Siegfried Gerhard
Hehner-Kiltz
J. F. Kimich
Knyphausen
Kruger-Rumpf
Lingenfelder
Theo Minges
Eugen Müller
Neckarauer
Jacob Riedel
Balthasar Ress
Schloss Eltz
Schloss Johannisberg
Schloss Schönborn
Schloss Vollrads

Jacob Schneider
Seebrich
von Simmern
Staatsweingut Eltville
J. & H. A. Strub
Domdechant Werner
Wegeler-Deinhard
Gunter Wittman

Baden
Baden, Franconia
Badischer
   Winzerkeller
Schwarzer Adler
Hans Wirsching
Wolff Metternich

Reliable Shippers and Importers

These names on German wines consistently indicate quality:

Deinhard
H. Sichel Söhne

A Terry Theise Estate
   Selection
Hans Wirsching

Selected Villages and Vineyards
of Superior Quality

NOTE: Villages always have "er" attached to the village name. The names following the village are vineyard, *Einzellage,* or a collective of superior vineyards *(Grosslage).* Best buys in brackets from certain producers.

Ayler: Kupp [Gebrüder Kramp]
Bad Kreuznacher: Brückes, Kahlenberg,
   Steinweg [Krönenberg]
Baden: Badischer Winzerkeller

Bernkasteler: Bereich [Sichel]

Bernkasteler: (Badstube Kurfürstlay)
[Wegeler-Deinhard ✪, Weins-Prüm,
Selbach-Oster, Friedrich Wilhelm, Vereinigte
Hospitien, Prüm, Sichel, Terry Theise
Selection, Bergweiler-Prüm]

Brauneberger: Juffer [W. Haag ✪, von
Kesselstatt, Richter]

Deidesheimer: Herrgottsacker, Leinhöhle,
Hohenmorgen (Mariengarten)
[Bassermann-Jordan, Bürklin-Wolf, von Buhl]

Eltviller: Sonnenberg, Taubenberg
[Staatsweingut, von Simmern]

Erbacher: Marcobrunn ♦ [Schönborn]

Erdener: Treppchen [W. Schwaab, Meulenhof,
Mönchhof, Bergweiler-Prüm, Christoffel]

Forster: Jesuitengarten, Kirchenstück
[Bassermann-Jordan, Bürklin-Wolf,
Deinhard]

Geisenheim: Rothenberg, Mönchspad
(Burgweg) [Deinhard, Zweirlein]

Graacher: Himmelreich, Josephshöfer ✪
[Thanisch, W. Schäfer Kabinett, von
Kesselstatt Kabinett ✪]

Hallgartener: Jungfer [Deinhard, Eser,
Siegfried Gerhard Kabinett]

Hattenheimer: Steinberg, Nussbrunnen [B. Ress
Kabinett, Schönborn]

Hochheimer: Domdechaney, Kirchenstück
[Deinhard, Ress, Schönborn]

Iphofener Franconia: Julius-Echter-Berg [Hans
Wirsching]

Johannisberger: Schloss Johannisberg [von
Metternich]

Kaseler: (Romerlay) [Karlsmuhle, von
Kesselstatt]

Niederhauser: Hermannshöhe [Staatsweingut,
Donnhoff, Hehner-Kiltz, J. Schneider]

Niersteiner: Hipping, Olberg [Deinhard, Strub]
Ockfener: Bockstein, Herrenberg [Deinhard
    Spätlese ✪, Dr. Fischer]
Oppenheimer: Sackträger (Guldenmorgen)
Piesporter: Goldtröpfchen, Falkenberg,
    Hofberger [Deinhard, von Kesselstatt
    Kabinett, Milz Kabinett, Moselland]
Rauenthaler: Baiken, Gehrn, Wulfen
    [Staatsweingut, von Simmern]
Rüdesheimer: Berg (Burgweg)
Ruppertsberger: Reiterpfad
    [Bassermann-Jordan, Bürklin-Wolf, von Buhl]
Scharzhofberger: [von Kesselstatt, Egon Müller ♦]
Schlossböckelheimer: Kupfergrube, Felsenberg
Urziger: Wurzgarten [Dr. Loosen, Mönchhof,
    Christoffel, Merkelbach]
Wachenheimer: Gerümpel, Rechbächel
    [Bürklin-Wolf]
Wehlener: Sonnenuhr [Wegeler-Deinhard,
    Kerpen, von Kesselstatt, Moselland, J. J.
    Prüm ♦]
Wiltinger: Braune, Kupp, Klosterberg [Le
    Gallais]
Winkeler: Hasensprüng, Jesuitengarten [Ress,
    Schönborn, Schloss Vollrads ♦,
    Wegeler-Deinhard]
Zeltinger: Himmelreich [Friedrich Wilhelm,
    Selbach-Oster]

Labels to Be Wary of Because of Quality Variation (exceptions are recommended shippers or importers)

Bereich Bernkasteler
Liebfraumilch (except Blue Nun, Hans Christof-
fel)
Niersteiner Gutes Domtal
Piesporter Michelsberg

Piesporter Treppchen
Zeller Schwarze Katz

SUPERBUYS / GERMANY

Graacher Josefshoffer Riesling Kabinett, von
   Kesselstatt, $11

Brauneberger Juffer Riesling Kabinett, Willi
   Haag, $11.99

Dienheimer Falkenberg Riesling Kabinett, Dr.
   Becker, $9

Erdener Treppchen, Meulenhof, $10

Ockfener Bockstein Riesling Spätlese, Dr.
   Fischer, $11

Rheingau Bereich Johannisberg Riesling, Sichel,
   $6.29

Bernkasteler Badstube Riesling Kabinett,
   Wegeler-Deinhard, $9.50; Selbach-Oster
   Kabinett, $9

Niersteiner Hipping Spätlese, Strub, $10

Deinhard Riesling QbA, $7

Zeltinger Himmelreich Halbtrocken, $8

Uerziger Wurzgarten, Christoffel, $11.50

Wehlener Sonnenuhr Kabinett, $10–12

Australia

When Australian wines hit the U.S. market some years ago, their bold, vivid flavors made a big impact on American wine drinkers. Full-bodied Chardonnays with lots of oak and flamboyant fruit won many fans, as did the dark, berryish reds known as Shiraz. Some Cabernet Sauvignons were leaner, a little harder to like, but for the price—mostly $5 to $8 or $10 a bottle—Americans were more than willing to experiment with wines from Down Under.

At that time the exchange rate for the Australian dollar was more favorable than now. Though a few wines from small Australian wineries were available, most of the wine shipped at that stage was from large wineries and moderately priced. Now the situation has changed somewhat. Australia's stronger currency has boosted prices, and American enthusiasm for Aussie wines encouraged exports of more expensive ones. Good buys under $10 are somewhat scarcer as a result of these factors, but some real bargains remain. American consumers have shown some resistance, in fact, to higher prices, so quite a few wines just over the limit can be found marked down (♦).

Australia's wine industry goes back some two hundred years, about the same time, give or take a few decades, that other New World wine regions (America, Chile, Argentina) were getting under way. As in those regions, it is the last two decades that have made all the difference in quality and style. Fast-growing and dynamic, the Australian wine industry now has some five hundred wineries, scattered across the southern half of the vast continent. There are many important growing regions—Hunter Valley, Barossa Valley, the Southern Vales, Coonawarra, Margaret River, and dozens more emerging into prominence.

Regions, however, are somewhat less important than varietal name and producer at this point—for American wine drinkers, at any rate. As in the California section, the wines are covered alphabetically by varietal, with a separate category for proprietary brands as well as for fortified and dessert wines. I have found that quality varies quite a bit with Australian wines, some of it due to still-evolving techniques in winemaking. Many of the large wineries have swallowed up smaller ones, and transitions in styles are still somewhat in flux. Only those wines that I have found to be consistently good are included here, but Australian exports have jumped tenfold in the last decade and continue to increase. As new labels appear, many of them may be well worth exploring, but it will be wise to exercise caution.

Cabernet Sauvignon

Cabernet is widely grown in Australia, ranging in style from wines that are rather firm, lean, and peppery in character to the richer, more intense versions flavored with essence of blackberry, cassis, and a good wallop of new oak. The costlier ones invariably need a few years of aging, as do the lean styles from the cool district of Coonawarra at the southern tip of South Australia. Less expensive Cabernets, usually intended for earlier drinking, are fruity and smooth, but on the whole Australian Cabernet is somewhat less generous than Shiraz, as well as more variable from vintage to vintage.

Age: Best at 3–5 years; sturdy ones can go 6, 8, even 10
Price: $7–10
Recommended Producers: Black Opal ✪, Brown Brothers Family Reserve ♦✳, Chateau Reynella, Château Tahbilk, Peter Lehmann ✪, Lindemans Bin 45, Mildara Coonawarra ✪, Rosemount Diamond, St. Hugo, Seaview, Seppelt, Taltarni ♦, Wirra Wirra McLaren Vale, Wolf Blass, Wynns
Foods: Roast or grilled lamb and beef

Cabernet/Shiraz or Shiraz/Cabernet

Shiraz is the name for the Syrah grape in Australia, which produces robust, berryish reds (see Shiraz). The blend of Cabernet Sauvignon and Shiraz yields Australia's most popular red wine, sort of the Zinfandel of Australia, usually moderately priced and widely used as a hearty pour for casual or everyday use. Some of these wines are wonderfully fruity and flavorful, especially those

that are predominantly Shiraz, such as Penfolds
Koonunga Hill Shiraz/Cabernet, a Superbuy, you
will note. Usually the varietal that is first domi-
nates in the blend. Some, however, are labeled
with proprietary names, such as Rosemount's Diamond Reserve Red, which is roughly half and
half and an excellent value (see Proprietary
Blends). Other grapes, such as Malbec and Merlot, may also be included in the blend and mentioned on the label.

Age: **Drinkable on release, or within 2–4 years;
   some are nonvintage**
Price: **$7–10**
Recommended Producers: **Balgownie, Cassegrain,
   Jacob's Creek, Mitchelton, Oxford Landing,
   Penfolds Koonunga Hill ☺, Seppelt, Wirra Wirra
   Church Block ♦, Wolf Blass, Wynn's Cabernet/
   Hermitage**
Foods: **Hearty barbecues, meat or game stews, goat
   cheese**

Chardonnay

Australian Chardonnays fairly burst with flavor,
with showy fruit that speaks of citrus or pineap-
ple, spices like clove, cinnamon, and vanilla, and
the rich, buttery character that comes from time
in new oak barrels. This rush of flavor quite cap-
tivated American wine drinkers, especially when
some of the top wines were going for $7 or $8
a bottle. Many of those Chardonnays now cost
upward of $12, though good values remain. A
number of wineries produce Chardonnays in various price categories. Quality variation at the
under-$10 level is considerable, and many of
these wines are too sweet for my taste. The bet-

ter ones, however, are well balanced with rich, opulent flavors that many Chardonnay lovers find irresistible. Be on the lookout for wines that are often marked down (♦). Perceptible sweetness is noted by the symbol ♥.

Age: 1–3 years

Price: $6.50–10 +

Recommended Producers: Angove's, Black Opal ♥, Brown Brothers E.B. ✳, Château Reynella ♦✪, Hardy (Bird Series), Lindemans Bin 65 ♥, Mitchellton, Penfolds, Rosemount Diamond Label, Rothbury Estate Brokenback ♦, Seaview, Seppelt Black Label, Tyrell's Vat 47 ✪, Yalumba

Foods: Can be overpowering with delicate or subtle foods, fine with spicy shellfish or grilled shrimp; less assertive ones go with fish, chicken, and pastas in cream sauce, wild mushrooms

Fumé Blanc, Sauvignon Blanc

As in California, the names are interchangeable for wines made from the Sauvignon Blanc grape. Australian Fumés are crisp and grassy, with citrusy flavors of lime more than lemon, perhaps because they all tend to be slightly sweet. Cold fermentation and high acidity give them lots of zing, though some are aggressively herbaceous and these are usually the ones that are sweetened a bit to modify sharpness and austerity.

New Zealand is coming on very strong with Sauvignon Blanc, from areas like Hawkes Bay and Marlborough. New Zealand Sauvignons tend to be pricey, however, except for a couple listed here (whose price tags are also inching up). New Zealand wines are followed by NZ in parentheses.

Age: Best at 1–2 years, can go 3
Price: $6–10 +
Recommended Producers: Angove's, Babich (NZ),
  Brown Brothers E.B., Corbans Marlborough (NZ)
  ✪, Hill-Smith Fumé, Morton Hawkes Bay (NZ),
  Roo's Leap Fumé, Rothbury Estate, Taltarni
Foods: Spicy seafood, especially shellfish, gravlax,
  goat cheese, salads with light vinaigrette or
  mustard dressing

Proprietary Blends

Inexpensive blends with proprietary or brand
names are very popular in Australia. The country's best-selling single wine, reportedly, is Tyrell's Long Flat Red, mostly Shiraz smacked with
Cabernet and Malbec. This hearty red used to go
for something like $2.99 in the United States,
but now is up to $4.50 or $5. Still a Superbuy.
Rosemount's Diamond Reserve Red, about half
Shiraz, half Cabernet, is also an excellent buy,
but the Diamond Reserve White is a Superbuy—
mainly Hunter Valley Sémillon with a dash of
Sauvignon Blanc to freshen it up. Both, however,
are a bit on the "mellow" side.

Age: Immediately drinkable
Price: $4–6.50
Recommended Producers: Hardy Premium Classic
  Dry Red and Dry White, Rosemount Diamond
  Reserve Red and White ✪, Tyrell's Long Flat Red
  ✪ and White

Rhine Riesling

The true German Riesling is called Rhine Riesling
in Australia, occasionally Johannisberg Riesling.

Riesling is produced in great quantities in Australia. Excellent Rieslings are made in the Barossa Valley and Coonawarra, fresh, flowery, delicate, and usually dry or off-dry. Relatively little is exported to the United States because Rieslings are not appreciated here, but perhaps we will see more good Australian Rieslings in the future. Luscious late-harvest Rieslings are also made; affordable ones are listed under dessert wines.

Age: 1–2 years, can go longer
Price: $5–10
Recommended Producers: Jacob's Creek ♥,
   Penfolds Green Ribbon, Pewsy Vale ✪, Wynn's
   Coonawarra ✪
Foods: Poached or broiled fish, smoked salmon,
   cold chicken or turkey, chicken salad, pasta
   primavera, steamed asparagus with hollandaise
   or vinaigrette

Semillon-Chardonnay

The white grape Semillon is not well known in the United States, particularly as a varietal, but it has long been one of Australia's most popular whites, and widely produced. The full-bodied, rich, oaky style of Semillon that is most favored was developed in the Hunter Valley (where it was once called, curiously enough, Hunter Riesling). In the United States and Bordeaux, Semillon is often blended with Sauvignon Blanc and is the principal grape used in Sauternes, but the style of Australian Semillon is unique. Ripe, full-flavored, somewhat honeyed in character, it served the role that Chardonnay played before it became widely planted in Australia. In the

United States we are more likely to see Semillon-Chardonnay than just Semillon. The two make a lively blend, often rounded off with a bit of sweetness, but in well-balanced wines this does not hinder their palate-pleasing flavors. More Chardonnay is imported from Australia than Semillon.

Age: **Drinkable young, but good ones may not hit flavor peak till 4 or 5 years, and hold a few beyond**
Price: **$5–10 +**
Recommended Producers: **Henschke, Lindemans, Penfolds Koonunga Hill, Rosemount ✪, Rothbury Estate, Tyrell's**

Shiraz

Shiraz, or Syrah, is sometimes labeled Hermitage in Australia in honor of the great Rhône red of that name. Shiraz is the Persian name for the Syrah grape, which is one of the world's oldest. Australia's world-famous (and most expensive) red, Penfolds Grange Hermitage, is made from Shiraz. The variety was first developed in the Hunter Valley, where producers tried for the robust, powerful, almost burnt flavor of the Rhône's biggest reds—sometimes resulting in very brawny, alcoholic wines. Shiraz is grown widely in Australia today, and the modern style is for ripe, full-bodied but not heavy reds, rich with the flavors of blackberries or cassis. This is especially true of moderate-priced Shiraz, which is often a remarkable bargain when the wines are good. More expensive ones, such as Taltarni ($12), tend to be dark, full-bodied, and tannic, needing a few years' aging to be drinkable.

Age: 3–5 years, sturdy ones in price range may go
    8–10
Price: $7–10
Recommended Producers: Brown Brothers, Leo
    Buring, Château Tahbilk, Hill-Smith, Jacob's
    Creek, Peter Lehmann ♥, Lindemans Bin 50,
    Montrose, Rosemount Diamond Label, Rothbury
    Estate, Saltram Hazlewood, Seaview, Seppelt
    Black Label, Taltarni Wynns
Foods: Lamb or beef stew, game, savory cheeses
    (goat cheese with the very berryish ones like
    Hill-Smith)

Shiraz/Cabernet (See Cabernet/Shiraz)

Dessert and Fortified Wines

Australia has a long tradition of flavorful dessert
and fortified wines, some of which are excellent
value. Many of the late-harvest Rieslings and
Semillons, usually possessing the honeyed flavors
of Botrytised (noble rot) grapes, are lusciously
sweet and well balanced. Dessert Muscats, such
as Brown Brothers Lexia or Mildara Moscat
Blanc, are exotic nectars that make a wonderful
finish to a meal.

The warm regions of central Australia, like the
Riverina district and regions along the Murray
River, produce excellent fortified wines, such
as the very fine and very drinkable Yalumba
Clocktower Port and Seppelt's Para Bin 110 Oloroso Sherry. In full bottles (750 milliliters), prices
for good Ports and Shery, as well as late-harvest
wines, have moved beyond $12, but many of
them are available in half-bottles (375 milliliters,
and so noted in the list below) that are well
within reach.

Age: Drinkable at release, but late-harvest wines
   can age several years
Price: $7–10
Recommended Producers: Brown Brothers Lexia ✪,
   Drayton's Pioneer Port, Heggies Botrytised Rhine
   Riesling (375), Peter Lehmann Vintage Port,
   Mildara Late Harvest Moscat Blanc, Penfolds
   Botrytised Semillon (375), Pewsey Vale Botrytised
   Riesling ✪ (375), Seppelt Para Bin 110 Oloroso
   Sherry, Seppelt Show Muscat, Yalumba
   Clocktower Port ✪ ♦

SUPERBUYS / AUSTRALIA
AND NEW ZEALAND

White

Lindemans Chardonnay Bin 65, Mitchellton
   Marsanne, $9
Seppelt Reserve Bin Chardonnay, $8.99
Penfolds Koonunga Hill Semillon/Chardonnay,
   $7.49
Rosemount Diamond Chardonnay, $7.50
Rosemount Chardonnay/Semillon, $7.50
Corbans Marlborough Sauvignon Blanc, $9–11
Pewsey Vale Riesling, $6
Wynn's Coonawarra Riesling, $6
Pewsey Vale Botrytised Riesling, $8.50
Brown Brothers Lexia Muscat, $7

Red

Penfolds Koonunga Hill Cabernet Shiraz, $7.49
Rosemount Diamond Reserve Red, $4.50
Tyrell's Long Flat Red, $4.50
Peter Lehmann Shiraz, $7
Montrose Shiraz, $7.99
Peter Lehmann Vintage Port, $9

SOUTH AFRICA

South African wines are finally making it to this country. They offer some very good values in both reds and whites. Quality has been steadily increasing since the midseventies as the country has become less isolated. South Africa's principal wine regions are in the Cape Province, which includes Stellenbosch, Constantia, and Paarl; Swartland to the west, and the Breede River Valley to the east. Chenin Blanc, locally known as Steen, is the predominant white grape, producing fresh, crisp whites ranging from dry to sweet. Off-dry versions are often excellent values. Chardonnay, Riesling, and Sauvignon Blanc are now more widely grown. The Rhône variety Cinsaut was long the peninsula's red grape, producing robust, hearty wines, but South Africa's unique contribution to wine is the Pinotage, a cross between Pinot Noir and Cinsaut. Styles of Pinotage range from very light and fruity to dark and meaty. The most immediately enjoyable, however, are somewhere in between, with good berryish fruit and solid structure that is very appealing. Vineyard expansion in recent years has included more Cabernet Sauvignon, Cabernet Franc, Merlot, and Syrah. Entries below reflect the types of wines in widest distribution here in the United States, sold at attractive introductory prices.

Cabernet Sauvignon

Cabernet is generally made in two or three styles by large wineries and co-ops: fruity, medium-bodied, barrel-aged for riper, more tannic wines and in blends with other varieties such as Merlot, Pinotage, and Shiraz.

Age: 2–5 years
Price: $5.99–12
Recommended Producers: Blaauwklippen,
Kanonkop ("Kadette"), Neethlingshof,
Rustenberg, Sable View, Springbok, Swartland,
Zonnebloem

Chardonnay

Brisk and lively, often with accents of citrus and oak. South African Chardonnays are somewhat lean but elegant, some quite oaky but rarely heavy or overly oaked.

Age: 2–4 years
Price: $5.99–11
Recommended Producers: Blaauwklippen, Glen
Carlou, Hamilton-Russell, Nederburg,
Neethlingshof, Sable View, Springbok, Swartland,
Zonnebloem

Chateau Libertas

A hearty, somewhat tannic blend of Cabernet, Cinsaut, Merlot, and Shiraz that is considered one of South Africa's best reds from the historic 1689 Oude Libertas estate. Best with rich meat dishes or game.

Chenin Blanc

Also known as Steen, the most widely planted white in South Africa. Made in a range of styles, from fresh, crisp, and dry to off-dry (listed below) to sweet and late-harvest. Generally light-bodied with good acidity and peachlike aromas.

Age: 1–2 years, sweet ones can last longer
Price: $4–8
Recommended Producers: Landskroon, Nederburg, Swartland

Edelrood

A Nederburg blend of Cabernet, Merlot, and Shiraz, this richly flavored red (*edelrood* means "noble red") goes superbly with duck, goose, grilled meats, and lamb.

KWV

South Africa's largest cooperative in the Stellenbosch region of the Cape Province; produces a broad range of red, white, pink, dessert, and fortified wines.

Nederburg

Most famous and one of the largest South African wineries situated in the Paarl Valley. Nederburg produces a broad range of wines, including several blends such as Baronne, a Cabernet blend and Edelrood, both good values.

Merlot

The few seen here so far are quite good but over $12. Look for the plummy, berryish Landskroon, which is under $10.

Pinotage

An excellent red, a cross of Pinot Noir and Cinsaut developed in South Africa. Good ones show the best of both, the fruitiness of Pinot and the structure of sturdy reds from the Rhône. Though some can be harsh and tannic, more balanced ones are fine drinking, especially with light game and grilled meats.

Age: 3–10 years, longer for bigger ones
Price: $9.95–12 +
Recommended Producers: Backsberg Clos Malverne, Cap du Fleur, Landskroon, Nederburg, Neethlingshof, Sable View, Simonsig, Springbok, Zonnebloem

Sauvignon Blanc

Lively and zesty in the style of Loire Sauvignons, with bright fruit and often a touch of oak.

Recommended: Boschendal, Mulderbosch, Neethlingshof, Sable View, Thelema, Zonnebloem

Sparkling Wines

Most wineshops group sparkling wines together, since consumers usually want to peruse what's available. We often buy these wines based on price and style rather than origin, so instead of listing them within each country I thought it more useful to make them a category on their own.

There are dozens of sparkling wines for $12 and under, but not many that I can recommend for consistently good quality. Probably the overall best category for such wines are the Spanish *cavas*, which are made using a modified version of the traditional Champagne method. Most are made from the native Spanish grapes, Parellada, Xarel-lo, and Macabeo; some include Chardonnay, and those that are 100 percent Chardonnay are more expensive.

Leading Champagne brands are at an all-time high, but some wineshops around the country bring in direct imports that can be inexpensive. Sparkling wines from the Loire, the Languedoc, the Jura, and Alsace can be quite good and a few are recommended below.

California has raised quality across the board for sparkling wines made by the *methode champenoise*—and several of the leading Champagne

houses now have facilities in California—Deutz,
Lanson, Moët, Mumm, Roederer, Taittinger,
among others. At full markup California sparkling wines range from about $13 to $25. At certain times, however, various brands can be
found marked down or featured as loss leaders
(♦) that put them occasionally within our range.
It's rare with any of the French-owned, but
such as Domaine Chandon, Korbel, Mirassou,
Shadow Creek, or Wente can be great value.
Recommended below are sparklers from various
parts of the world and the United States, all of
which are dry except Asti (sweet Muscat from
Italy's Piedmont) and Ballatore (Gallo's lightly
sweet, semi-sparkling Muscat).

Age: Immediately drinkable
Price: $7–10 +
Recommended Producers: Ballatore ✪, Bouvet Brut
    ♦, Brut Pecher, Chase-Limogère, Cinzano Asti
    Spumante, Codorníu Brut Classico ✪ and Blanc
    de Blancs, Charles de Fere, Freixenet Brut Natur,
    Frescobaldi Brut, Gancia Pinot di Pinot and
    Gancia Asti ♦, Glenora Blanc de Blancs,
    Gratien & Meyer Brut and Blanc de Noir,
    Langlois Crémant Brut, Lembey Brut ✪ and
    Premiere Cuvée ♦, Marqués de Monistrol, Masia
    Brut, Monmousseau Sparkling Vouvray ♦,
    Mont-Marçal, Château Ste. Michelle Brut, Segura
    Viudas Blanc de Blanc, Valdivieso, Varichon &
    Clerc Savoir, Willm Crémant d'Alsace

Glossary

Included here are brief explanations of some of the terms used in the text.

Auslese. German for late-harvest, usually Botrytis-affected grapes that produce luscious sweet wines.

Beerenauslese. Rare and expensive late-harvest sweet wine from bunch-selected grapes.

Blanco, branco. Spanish and Portuguese for white wine.

Botrytis cinerea. The mold that forms on grapes during harvest to produce luscious sweet wines; also known as "noble rot."

Cépage. Grape variety.

Clarete. Spanish for light red.

Crianza. Young wines aged only a year or two in cask; *sin crianza* signifies unaged wines.

Flash pasteurizing. Subjecting a wine to a "flash" of high heat to prevent bacterial spoilage.

Garrafeira. Portuguese term for "personal or proprietor's reserve." Must be aged two years in wood, one in bottle before the wine is released.

Goût de terroir. French for the distinctive taste from a particular region or vineyard.

Grip. Wine-tasting term for a wine that has a firm thrust of fruit and tannin.

Halbtrocken, Trocken. Trocken is bone-dry, *Halbtrocken* is dry or half dry in Germany.

Kabinett. Dry or off-dry German wines.

Négociant. Shipper or company who buys grapes or wine and sells under a brand name.

Plonk. Nondescript everyday wine.

Prädikat. The highest quality category for German wines, those with natural sweetness: Kabinett, Auslese, Beerenauslese, Trockenbeerenauslese.

Proprietary. Wines from a single proprietor, often with a brand name.

Qualitätswein. German term meaning "quality wine," but it's the designation for average to good wine.

Quinta. Portuguese for estate (*herdade* used in Alentejo).

Reserva, Gran Reserva. Spanish for superior wines, aged longer in cask and/or bottle.

Riserva. Italian for Reserve wines made from better lots and aged longer.

Rosado, Rosato. Rosé wine.

Rosso. Red wine

Spätlese. Late harvest.

Tinto. Red wine.

Trockenbeerenauslese. Top quality level for rare, sweet German wines.

A Few Good Shops

Good wineshops and conscientious wine merchants have multiplied dramatically in the last decade. I have visited a good many and am on the mailing list of others, in an effort to keep track of wines available around the country. The following list is a selection of stores that I know personally to specialize in wine, offering diversity, good value, and good service. There are others, of course; I have not been to every state. Your local wineshop may well deserve to be here. But these stores are prototypes that typify the best in their area and are worth a visit if you are in the vicinity.

Atlanta: Happy Herman's; Harry's Farmers' Market
Berkeley: Kermit Lynch
Boston: Brookline Liquor Mart; Cirace & Son
Chicago: Sam's Wine Warehouse; Schaefer's (Skokie); Knightsbridge
Covington, Ky.: Cork 'n Bottle
Dallas: Marty's
Detroit: Merchant of Vino
Fort Lauderdale: Crown Liquor
Ho-Ho-Kus, N.J.: Wine & Spirit World
Honolulu: Vintage Wine Cellar

Houston: Richard's; Speck's

Kansas City, Mo.: Berbiglia; Gomer's

Los Angeles: Wally's; Trader Joe; Duke of Bourbon; Hi-Time Cellars (Costa Mesa); Wine Warehouse

Memphis: Arthur's; Buster's

Miami: Sunset Corners

Minneapolis: Haskell's

New Orleans: Martin Wine Cellar

New York City: Astor Wines & Spirits; Crossroads; Garnet; K & D; Morrell & Co.; Sherry-Lehmann; Heights Cellars (Brooklyn); Goldstar (Queens); Van Vleck (Brooklyn)

Westchester: Zachy's (Scarsdale); Rockwood & Perry (Hastings-on-Hudson)

Long Island: Pop's (Long Beach); Young's (Manhassett)

Upstate: Barbara's World (Albany); Century (Rochester); Premier Center (Buffalo)

Phoenix: Newman's Liquor Barn (Scottsdale)

Providence, R.I.: Town Wine and Spirits

Sacramento: Corti Bros.

St. Louis: Wine Cellar

San Francisco: The Jug Shop; Draper & Esquin; The Wine Club; Cost Plus; Pacific Wine Co.

Bay Area: Beltramo's (Menlo Park); Mill Valley Market

Santa Barbara: Wine Cask

Seattle: Larry's Markets; Thriftway

Springfield, Mo.: Brown Derby

Washington, D.C.: MacArthur's; Pearson's; Calvert Woodley; Mayflower

Index